The
CARRIAGE
Collection

The CARRIAGE *Collection*

THE MUSEUMS AT STONY BROOK

This publication was made possible by a grant from the National Endowment for the Humanities, a Federal agency.

The Museums at Stony Brook

Editorial Assistance by Alison Kilgour
Design by Melanie Roher Design, Inc.
Photography by Lynton Gardiner, unless otherwise noted
Black and white lab services by Kenneth S. Taranto, New
Jersey, unless otherwise noted
Color lab services by Cosmic Sound-Delight, New York
Typography by Centennial Graphics, Inc.
Printed by Eastern Press, Inc.

Published by The Museums at Stony Brook
1208 Route 25A
Stony Brook, New York 11790

CONTENTS

9   Foreword

13   Collecting Carriages at The Museums at Stony Brook

18   The Carriage Era

The Collection:

20   *European Vehicles*

28   *Personal Transportation in Pre-Industrial America*

36   *Personal Transportation in Industrial America*

48   *The Gypsy Wagon*

50   *Coachman-Driven Vehicles*

62   *Pleasure Driving Vehicles*

84   *Sleighs*

94   *Freight and Trade Vehicles*

104 *Public Transportation*

116 *Fire-Fighting Vehicles*

Appendixes:

122 *Major Parts of a Vehicle*

123 *Springs*

124 *Glossary*

126 *Further Readings*

127 *Index to Vehicles*

FOREWORD

Fashionable "Turn-outs" in Central Park, *1869*
Thomas Worth, artist; Currier and Ives, publisher;
New York, New York; Museums Collection

The carriage collection at The Museums at Stony Brook is predominantly an American collection, representative of most of the vehicle types used in the Carriage Era in the United States. Because European carriages were imported and used in America from the earliest days through the height of the Era in the late nineteenth century, a small but significant part of the collection is European. These vehicles contribute to the comprehensiveness of the collection.

This publication presents photographs and detailed descriptions of 80 vehicles, more than a third of The Museums collection; it is intended to be as representative of the collection as possible, and, as a collection catalog, omits information that might be found in a manual on carriage driving or a definitive history of horse-drawn transportation. Although a handful of scholars have made significant contributions in the field of carriage history and terminology in the past two decades, the subject has received little academic or popular attention since the end of the Carriage Era. Primary resources for such studies exist in tax records and in the archives of many corporations, libraries and museums across the country, including those in the Carriage Reference Library at The Museums. Research projects sponsored by The Museums during the last three years have just begun to reveal the wealth of information that is contained in such records. Much remains to be done on the history of the development and manufacture of horse-drawn vehicles, patterns of ownership and use and the role of horse-drawn transportation in the social and economic history of the United States.

In the preparation of this catalog, information was derived or verified by the use of collections records and correspondence from donors and a number of standard books and periodicals, many dating from the end of the nineteenth century. Information derived from more than one of these sources is not cited by source; additional references are cited in footnotes. The standard sources consulted include:

Adams, William Bridges. *English Pleasure Carriages: their Origin, History, Varieties, Materials, Construction.* London: Charles Knight & Co., 1837.

Berkebile, Don H. *Carriage Terminology: An Historical Dictionary.* Washington, D.C.: Smithsonian Institution Press & Liberty Cap Books, 1978.

The Carriage Journal, Salem, N.J.: the Carriage Association of America, issues from 1963 to 1985.

Dunbar, Seymour. *A History of Travel in America.* Indianapolis: The Bobbs-Merrill Company, 1915.

Garland, James A. *The Private Stable: Its Establishment, Management and Appointment.* Boston: Little, Brown and Co., 1903.

The Hub. New York: The Hub Publishing Company, issues dating from 1877 to 1896.

The New York Coachmakers Magazine. New York: Ezra M. Stratton, issues from 1858 to 1861.

Stratton, Ezra M. *The World on Wheels, or Carriages with their Historical Associations from the Earliest to the Present Time.* New York: Ezra M. Stratton, 1878.

Underhill, Francis T. *Driving For Pleasure; or the Harness Stable and its Appointments.* New York: D. Appleton and Company, 1896.

Ware, Francis M. *Driving.* New York: Doubleday, Page & Company, 1903.

The sources used also include unpublished manuscripts, among them twelve notebooks prepared by Paul Downing for Ward Melville in 1954 and correspondence between Richard Gipson and Ward Melville from 1944 to 1962.

These sources are contained in The Museums Carriage Reference Library or in The Museums institutional archives.

The authors are grateful to the following for research assistance for this book: C. Cretors and Company, Chicago, Illinois (Charles Cretors); Discovery Hall Museum, South Bend, Indiana (Geoffrey Huys); Gladys L. Hawks, Springfield, Massachusetts; Henry Ford Museum and Greenfield Village, Dearborn, Michigan (Randy Mason); Maryland Historical Society, Baltimore, Maryland (Sally Mason); The Metropolitan Museum of Art, New York, New York (Janet S. Byrne and Mary L. Myers); National Museum of American History, Smithsonian Institution, Washington, D.C. (Matt Salo); New Bedford Free Public Library, New Bedford, Massachusetts (Paul Cyr); The New-York Historical Society, New York, New York (Cammie Naylor); Rare Books and Manuscripts Division, New York Public Library, New York, New York.

The authors are indebted to the following individuals for assistance in verifying information and in the review of this manuscript: Don H. Berkebile, Associate Curator of Transportation (retired), National Museum of American History; Thomas Ryder, carriage historian and editor of *The Carriage Journal*; Richard E. Slavin, III, historian and museum consultant; and past and present members of The Museums Carriage Collection Advisory Committee. This publication could not have been completed without their substantial assistance. Generous funding and intellectual encouragement were provided by the National Endowment for the Humanities, a Federal agency, for the publication of a two-volume book about carriages: this volume—a collection catalog—and a companion volume about aspects of the history of carriages in nineteenth-century America.

A Guide to the Catalog

The introductory chapter presents the history of The Museums extraordinary carriage collection and the collecting interests of its founder, Ward Melville, and places the formation of the collection in the historic context of a collecting tradition in America. Another chapter defines the Carriage Era. The remainder of the catalog consists of photographs and descriptions of 80 vehicles, chosen as the best examples in the collection of vehicle types used during all periods of the Carriage Era. Vehicles were selected on the basis of representative types and arranged according to the date of manufacture or historic function.

The catalog descriptions are divided into major groups: European vehicles, early American vehicles, those used for personal transportation, those that were coachman-driven, pleasure vehicles, sleighs, trade vehicles, public transportation and fire-fighting vehicles. The Gypsy wagon, representative of a kind of vehicle used by a distinct cultural group in the United States, is presented in a separate category. Space did not permit the inclusion of children's vehicles, whether functional or toys, although a number of them are in The Museums collection. The beginning of each section contains a brief history of the vehicle type and discusses representative vehicles of that type whether or not they are in The Museums collection.

The information about each vehicle is arranged in a specific sequence to assist the reader in comparing vehicles in this and in other collections:

Vehicle Name: When known, the name of the vehicle is that used by the manufacturer or the name most commonly used in the literature of the period; vehicle names are not capitalized in this catalog. Other commonly-used names are included in the descriptive text. The complexities of carriage terminology are historic: carriage makers often created new names for vehicles to differentiate their products from those of competing manufacturers, and local names and the names of clients who were instrumental in the design of a specific carriage were also used. Translation of names from one language to another in the case of imported vehicles has added to the confusion. Sir Walter Gilbey, in his 1905 book *Modern Carriages*, noted that "The difficulty of dividing carriages into distinct groups or classes has increased during the last half century or more, owing to the ingenuity of coachmakers who have contrived to make one carriage adaptable for various purposes."[1]

Maker: The name of the carriage maker or the manufacturing company is entered when known, along with the address for that date. When this information is lacking, attribution has been made to the country of origin.

Date: The actual date of manufacture is used. When unknown, the date is approximated after verification with standard sources and consultants.

Dimensions: Dimensions are listed by length, width and height, in that order, and are given to the nearest inch and centimeter. Length measurements are from the outer edges of wheels unless the body or parts of the undercarriage extend beyond the wheels. Width is measured hub to hub and height is the measurement from the ground to the highest point on the vehicle. Length measurements do not include the dimensions of shafts or poles since these are removable parts and it cannot always be verified that they are original to a vehicle.

Condition: Each vehicle is described in terms of original, restored or conserved condition, with the exact or probable date of the treatment applied, in order to assist the reader in assessing the condition of the vehicles in other collections. The Museums makes the distinction between restoration and conservation, addressing very recent developments in collections care in the museum profession.

Restoration, a common practice of both private collectors and museums for much of the twentieth century, often involves the partial or total removal of original materials that have been altered or damaged by time and wear and the replacement of these by modern materials. Restoration results are sometimes influenced as much by personal preference as by an attempt to restore the vehicle as closely as possible to its original appearance. Although many vehicles in The Museums collection are in original condition, many others have been restored by previous owners or during the early years of collections care at The Museums.

New scientific procedures in object conservation are now revealing unexpected evidence about paint colors, decoration and trim used by vehicle manufacturers during the Carriage Era, making many early assumptions in restoration practice obsolete. Often, too, the paints, glazes, textiles and other materials originally used in carriage-making are now difficult or impossible to obtain and prohibitively expensive to reproduce accurately.

The Museums collections care policy currently establishes that conservation is the treatment of choice in the care of objects, including horse-drawn vehicles. The objective is to preserve whatever remains of original paint, glazes and carved and applied decoration, and to take other measures that will stabilize and protect original finishes from further deterioration.

Such conservation techniques, already accepted in the field of fine and decorative arts, have only recently been applied to the care of horse-drawn vehicles. Since 1980, The Museums has supported innovative work in carriage conservation, recognizing that original finishes survive as irreplaceable documents of the Carriage Era.

Credits: Here are listed the names of donors of each vehicle and the dates of their gifts to The Museums. Museum purchases are listed when appropriate.

Description: Each vehicle is described in a consistent manner, beginning with the characteristics that make the vehicle unusual or typical within its historical type. Following this is a description of the construction and finish of the exterior, then of the interior and finally of the undercarriage, suspension system and spring types used. Some contemporary terms for trim fabrics and other materials are indicated with quotation marks to avoid confusion with more modern meanings. The last section deals with provenance, the history of the vehicle's ownership and use.

Where serial number, maker's marks, monograms and heraldic symbols exist, they are included in the appropriate description and defined if the information has been verified. Serial numbers appear in a variety of places on a vehicle, generally stamped in the wood. Descriptions lacking such information indicate that no such marks were found during careful examination of the visible parts of the vehicle.

This catalog was designed with a variety of readers in mind, from the casual museum visitor to the history enthusiast, and including private collectors as well as scholars and those responsible for carriage collections in other museums. The authors hope to demonstrate that horse-drawn vehicles, like other perhaps more familiar artifacts, are objects of cultural interest, historical importance and beauty. The Museums also hopes to promote wider acceptance of conservation techniques in the care of horse-drawn vehicles and to encourage new research efforts on these complex, fascinating and rare survivals.

---

[1]Sir Walter Gilbey, *Modern Carriages*, London: Vinton and Co., 1905.

COLLECTING CARRIAGES
At The Museums at Stony Brook

The extraordinary collection of horse-drawn vehicles at The Museums at Stony Brook was begun by Ward Melville, a man fascinated by the past and committed to public education. He began in the early 1940s to collect the works of Stony Brook's nineteenth-century artist William Sidney Mount; by the mid-1940s, he was collecting carriages. Mr. Melville's interest in collecting paintings and artifacts related to America's past was part of a trend of interest in American history and artifacts that began in the late nineteenth century and developed rapidly in the twentieth century.

During most of the nineteenth century, American collectors of art and antiques collected primarily European works. Late in the century several collectors began to collect American art and antiques. From that time, and during the first decades of the twentieth century, a number of collectors gathered objects that today form the bases of major public collections of American art and artifacts. Within the general framework of an interest in American history, these collectors had specific interests that led them along different paths. Some, like Henry Mercer and Henry Ford, were particularly interested in technology—the inventions and machines that assisted America's development as an industrialized nation. Others were fascinated with art, both fine and folk: Henry Francis du Pont collected examples of the finest American artistry displayed in craftsmanship in silver, furniture, ceramics and textiles. Electra Havemeyer Webb collected the works of less sophisticated, usually anonymous artists—the folk art of the American past such as decoys, quilts and pottery. Some collectors began, as did Ward Melville, with an interest in local or regional history.

In the 1860s and 1870s there was only occasional interest shown in American antiques, notably at the 1864 Brooklyn Sanitary Fair, held to raise funds for the care of wounded Union soldiers in the Civil War. Several historical curiosities were exhibited there, most of them associated with famous people.

During the 1880s a colonial revival occurred in the United States. It was reflected in

Ward Melville in the Carriage House, Stony Brook, New York, 1950s

architecture, in furniture—including factory-made colonial-style furniture—and in interior decoration. One theory about this late-nineteenth-century emergence of interest in the country's early history is that many Americans felt the need to establish their superiority over the increasing number of immigrants entering the United States—a superiority based on the supposed greater "American-ness" of the descendants of earlier immigrants to the North American shores. Another manifestation of this attitude was the establishment of organizations requiring personal descent from early European settlers, such as the Daughters of the American Revolution, the Sons of the American Revolution and the Colonial Dames of America.

Among the few American collectors who ventured away from European art and antiques, the focus was on decorative arts, such as fine furniture, ceramics and silver. An exception was Edward Lamson Henry (1841–1919), a successful painter who was also a collector. After an 1887 auction of his collection of fine antiques, Henry appears to have focused his attention on collecting carriages and costumes, which he portrayed in his nostalgic paintings that re-created scenes of early-nineteenth-century daily life. Some of his carriages and paintings are now in The Museums collection. Upon Henry's death in 1919, *The New York Evening Post* published in his obituary the statement, "Without claiming for Mr. Henry a dominant place, there are few artists who have better served their country in preserving for the future the quaint and provincial aspects of a life which has all but disappeared since we have become the melting pot of other races than our own."[1]

Another collector who focused his energies on collecting artifacts of the everyday life of early America was Henry Chapman Mercer (1856–1930), of Doylestown, Pennsylvania, an archaeologist and scholar. He began collecting hand tools in 1897, considering them to be representative of a rapidly disappearing way of life: "Because they came to an end so suddenly and so near our own lives, they are still within reach, but they are vanishing fast, and we must gather them together now or never."[2] Among the artifacts Mercer collected were several vehicles, including a conestoga wagon. Although the conestoga wagon's primary use was as a freight wagon, particularly in Pennsylvania, during the eighteenth and nineteenth centuries, Mercer characterized the vehicle as "standing for the whole westward march of the Anglo-Saxon colonization, and the transportation of all merchandise over mountains and plains toward the setting sun, before the birth of railroads."[3] In 1914–1916 Mercer built a museum to house his collection. The building, made of poured reinforced concrete for fire protection, was opened as a museum in 1916 and is today a part of The Bucks County Historical Society.

During the first few decades of the twentieth century the collecting of American antiques ceased to be the exclusive realm of a few private individuals as museums became interested in collecting and exhibiting fine American decorative arts. In 1909 a temporary exhibition of American decorative arts at The Metropolitan Museum of Art—part of the festivities held to celebrate Robert Fulton's first successful steamboat trip in 1807 and the discovery and exploration of the Hudson River—was a major success, viewed by over 300,000 visitors. This exhibition was the beginning of a continuing commitment by major museums to collect and display American decorative arts. In 1924 The Metropolitan Museum of Art opened the first American Wing, featuring 16 period rooms. In 1929 The Brooklyn Museum opened 12 period rooms. On September 22, 1929, Malcolm Vaughan commented in the *Herald Tribune*, "This Americana passion is so widespread as to be an epidemic rage."[4]

Several historical museums that today are known throughout the country for their marvelous collections of American artifacts—The Henry Francis du Pont Winterthur Museum, the Shelburne Museum and the Henry Ford Museum and Greenfield Village—all began in the first third of the twentieth century as private collections. The Winterthur Museum collection was started in the mid-1920s with Henry Francis du Pont's interest in fine American decorative arts. After seeing the period rooms of The Metropolitan Museum of Art's American Wing, he decided to decorate his country house in Winterthur, Delaware, with period rooms representing the best quality craftsmanship in architecture and the decorative arts. He opened his house as a museum in 1951. The Shelburne Museum began as the private collection of Electra Havemeyer Webb, daughter of the Henry O. Havemeyers, who were themselves passionate collectors of nineteenth-century European art. Electra Webb, as a teenager, began collecting American folk art—the works of everyday Americans of the past. In 1947 she acquired all of the family carriages from a member of her husband's family, which included the Vanderbilts and the Webbs of Vermont; this was the impetus for founding a museum to exhibit the carriages and the rest of her extensive collection of Americana. The museum opened in 1952.

One of the most interesting collectors of this period was Henry Ford. Producer of the Model T Ford automobile, he gave to many Americans a mobility they had not previously had, and in so doing introduced an extraordinarily pervasive change in the life-styles of Americans and in the American landscape. While his products were changing the basic fabric of American life, Ford, even before 1920, began to collect the stuff of an American way of life that would soon disappear under the impact of widespread industrialization and the roads demanded by his automobiles. One of Ford's well-remembered reported comments was, "History is bunk." It appears ironical, therefore, that he would amass one of the greatest collec-

tions of objects relating to American history. But Ford concluded that the history that was then taught in the schoolroom, and in collected artifacts, told only the story of the elite and ignored the life of the common man. In 1928 he remarked to an acquaintance about his own collection, "All the relics have one thing in common: they are all things used by run-of-the-mill people, not by the elite. This is history, but not the history we get in textbooks where somebody cuts off somebody's head. The everyday lives of ordinary folk have been overlooked by historians who paid too much attention to violent and sensational events."[5]

Ford collected voraciously during the late 1910s and 1920s, often buying entire collections, and in 1929 opened his museum and outdoor village, the Edison Institute, more familiarly known as the Henry Ford Museum and Greenfield Village.

Ward Melville represents the next generation in collecting after du Pont, Webb and Ford. He began collecting in the early 1940s. The Melville family moved to Old Field, on the north shore of Long Island, in 1900, when Ward Melville was thirteen years old. The Frank Melvilles were interested in the local community; Ward Melville carried on their interests. About 1940, with the support and assistance of his wife, Dorothy Bigelow Melville, he launched a Stony Brook revitalization project whose aim was to build a new village center in a federal style.

Mr. and Mrs. Melville also became involved in supporting a small local museum, a collection of natural-history specimens that was chartered by New York State in 1942 as the Suffolk Museum. Mr. Melville's interest in local history led him to begin collecting for display in the museum the works of William Sidney Mount, a nineteenth-century Stony Brook artist who had been famous at home and abroad in his own time but had—with almost all other nineteenth-century American artists—fallen out of popularity in the twentieth century. Mr. Melville collected Mount's paintings and drawings—most of them of local scenes—as well as objects that had belonged to Mount and his family. Assisting Mr. Melville in his art collecting was Richard McCandless Gipson, described by Mr. Melville as "a non-resident curator engaged in securing material for the museum collection,"[6] whose connoisseurship and talent for patient negotiation significantly contributed to the development of Mr. Melville's superb collection. Mr. Gipson had lived in New York City and worked for The New-York Historical Society before moving to Old Field in 1943; shortly thereafter, he began to work for Mr. Melville.

Mr. Gipson suggested to Mr. Melville that he might be interested in collecting carriages, observing in a letter to Mr. Melville, "Fine carriages in good condition are becoming increasingly rare. We know how automobiles have driven them off the streets, and leaky barns and neglect have relegated all too many to extinction."[7] By 1949 Mr. Gipson could write to Mr. Melville, "Again I say that your collection is fast becoming the most important in the country."[8] In that same year, Mr. Gipson pointed out to Mr. Melville, "Now that you already have so many fine carriages, I think a very careful selective process should be followed. However, you may be able to replace a certain few of your carriages with better examples. In this event, I may be able to sell or trade the ones you would dispose of."[9] Early in the formation of the collection, the guiding principle was to have the best examples of various types of vehicles, and the growth of the collection included the practice of upgrading by obtaining a better example of a type of vehicle already in the collection and disposing of the lesser example. From the beginning of this new collecting venture, Mr. Melville aimed to make the carriage collection "thoroughly representative of various types of carriages."[10]

As with his art collection, Mr. Melville always planned to exhibit his carriage collection to the public. The growing collection was stored in the late 1940s in barns at Richard Gipson's residence in Old Field, and was exhibited to the public there on one occasion—on September 10, 1950, during a tour of historic sites that was sponsored by the Society for the Preservation of Long Island Antiquities, another organization in which Mr. Melville participated actively. In the same year, working with the architect Richard Haviland Smythe, he began plans for converting the deteriorating Stony Brook Hotel building, situated half a mile away from the Suffolk Museum building, into an annex for housing and displaying the carriage collection.

On Saturday, July 6, 1951, the new carriage museum opened with a day-long festival to celebrate the occasion. Eighty of the 125 vehicles in the collection were exhibited in the new facility. The collection now included vehicles Mr. Melville had purchased or been given as well as a number of vehicles donated to the museum by other institutions or individuals. For example, a Wells Fargo coach was donated by the Railway Express Agency, and many vehicles were donated by various Long Island families. The collection included not only horse-drawn vehicles, but accoutrements, such as harness, and a library of carriage-related volumes, pamphlets and prints. Mr. Gipson was particularly interested in establishing a carriage reference library as a resource of information about the vehicles: "This material is really scarce, so I am ever on the lookout for it."[11]

Following the 1951 opening of the carriage museum, the collection continued to grow both by purchase and by gift. As private stables were demolished and their contents dispersed, and some museums with vehicles in their collections decided they could no longer house them, additional gifts were made to the new carriage museum. Among the major institutional donors were The Society for the Preservation of New England Antiquities, The Farmers Museum in Cooperstown and the Johnstown Historical Society. The latter

Richard McCandless Gipson, Old Field, Setauket, New York, c. 1950

donated several carriages collected by Edward Lamson Henry. Many individuals donated their family vehicles or carriages they had collected.

In 1952 the Carriage Museum was physically expanded by the addition of a new wing. In 1954 a catalog of the carriage collection was published, with illustrations and detailed information on the vehicles. By 1956 Mr. Gipson wrote to Mr. Melville: "Before 1953, we had been building the basic collection. Since that time, I have been endeavoring to perfect the collection and to search the country exhaustively for rare and early vehicles. Your collection now numbers many rare vehicles and holds its position as the finest and most comprehensive collection in the country. . . . Each vehicle or each group of vehicles has been acquired with a definite purpose, for at all times I have had a well-defined goal of the comprehensive collection before me."[12]

As the collection's reputation spread, many requests for information were received by the museum. A list of these correspondents was kept, and in 1960 Mr. Melville invited them to come to the museum to see the collection. The meeting resulted in the founding of the Carriage Association of America, now an international organization of more than 3,000 members.

Mr. Gipson moved to Vermont in 1954, but continued to serve at long distance as the Melvilles' agent until his death in 1962. The carriage collection continued to develop thereafter under the guidance of the Melvilles and through the generosity of numerous donors.

In 1974 the name of the Suffolk Museum and Carriage House was changed to The Museums at Stony Brook. After Ward Melville's death in 1977, The Museums trustees, staff, and particularly curator George Isles and his successor Merri Ferrell, continued to maintain Melville's goals for this important carriage collection. A rigorous long-range planning program in the early 1980s identified the urgent need for a new carriage museum building to house more safely and exhibit more interpretively this extraordinary collection. The publication of this new catalog of the collection—the first since 1954—marks the occasion of the opening of the new carriage museum to exhibit the collection that owes its existence to Ward Melville's vision of capturing a portion of the American past and Richard Gipson's assistance and skill in pursuing that vision.

[1]Will Low, in *The New York Evening Post*, 12 May, 1919, quoted in Elizabeth McCausland, *The Life and Work of Edward Lamson Henry, N.A. 1841–1919* (Albany: New York State Museum Bulletin Number 339, University of the State of New York, 1945) 65.

[2]Henry C. Mercer, "The Tools of the Nation Maker," *A Collection of Papers Read Before The Bucks County Historical Society*, Vol. 3 (The Bucks County Historical Society, Riegelsville, Pennsylvania, 1919) 477.

[3]Mercer, 477.

[4]*The New York Herald Tribune*, 22 September 1929, quoted in Wendy Cooper, *In Praise of America: American Decorative Arts 1650–1830* (New York: Alfred A. Knopf, 1980) 4.

[5]William Greenleaf, *From These Beginnings: The Early Philanthropies of Henry and Edsel Ford, 1911–1936* (Detroit: Wayne State University Press, 1964) 16.

[6]Ward Melville, Letter to George Cray, February 13, 1959, ms., The Museums at Stony Brook.

[7]Richard McCandless Gipson, Letter to Ward Melville, September 27, 1949, ms., The Museums at Stony Brook.

[8]Richard McCandless Gipson, Letter to Ward Melville, October 25, 1949, ms., The Museums at Stony Brook.

[9]Richard McCandless Gipson, Letter to Ward Melville, November 2, 1949, ms., The Museums at Stony Brook.

[10]Ward Melville, Letter to Mr. and Mrs. Henry Taylor, October 24, 1949, ms., The Museums at Stony Brook.

[11]Richard McCandless Gipson, Letter to Ward Melville, October 25, 1949, ms., The Museums at Stony Brook.

[12]Richard McCandless Gipson, Letter to Ward Melville, March 16, 1956, ms., The Museums at Stony Brook.

THE CARRIAGE ERA

The Carriage Era, characterized by the widespread use of horse-drawn vehicles for personal and public transportation, began in the late seventeenth century in Europe. The era ended some 200 years later with the invention of the automobile. During those centuries a large number and wide variety of horse-drawn vehicles were developed and produced in both Europe and the United States.

Since its domestication, circa 3000 B.C., the horse—the source of power for horse-drawn transportation—has been an integral part of civilization. Although many early societies used it as a food resource, in time it became apparent that the horse, with its specific physical characteristics of speed and power and its tractability, was better utilized as a riding or draft animal.

Over the centuries, many breeds of horses were developed and improved for specific tasks and performance potential. The diminutive and hardy pony, which evolved under severe conditions, was used for diverse work, including hauling coal in mines, and was the ideal equine for children. Larger draft animals were used for hauling, land cultivation and other types of heavy work. The fast-trotting Standardbred was well suited to the lightweight American road wagon, racing sulky and buggy. Breeds such as the Cleveland Bay were sometimes used for pulling heavy coaches. The high-stepping Hackney, popular in the United States by the late nineteenth century, was preferred for the show ring. Certain mixed-breed or "grade" horses, which were steady, even-tempered and generally inexpensive, were favored by owners of all-purpose, utilitarian vehicles. For work or pleasure, the horse provided the necessary mobile force for transportation.

Horses were combined in various ways to perform their role as the external source of energy for vehicles. Of these, the single (one horse), pair (two horses abreast) and four-in-hand were the most common, although tandem (one horse hitched in front of the other), unicorn (one horse hitched in front of a pair) and other combinations were also used. The various ways in which horses were attached to a vehicle, as well as the specific size, breed or color, were intended to meet the requisites of the style of the vehicle and maximum efficiency in mobilizing it.

In the ancient civilizations of the Western world, horse-drawn chariots were used for war, for sport and for ceremony. Two-wheel carts and four-wheel wagons, often pulled by oxen, were used for hauling freight; their use for this purpose continues up to the present day in some parts of the world. For many centuries, however, people traveled by water when possible, and overland travel was on foot or on horseback. There is evidence that horse-drawn vehicles were sometimes used for personal transportation in Europe during the Middle Ages, and during the course of the sixteenth century members of European royal families began to travel for short distances in large, enclosed vehicles called coaches. By the seventeenth century the European aristocracy had begun to follow suit, and at the end of that century even the royal governors of the American colonies were riding in coaches imported from Europe.

During the eighteenth century roads were somewhat improved in both Europe and North America, although they remained quite crude in comparison to twentieth-century standards and in many areas were virtually inaccessible to vehicular traffic. Technological improvements in carriage design made traveling more comfortable for the passengers, and vehicles were now available in larger numbers and in a greater variety of forms. Ownership and maintenance of a carriage, however, continued to be a relatively expensive undertaking. For the majority, land transportation continued to be on foot or on horseback or by one of the forms of horse-drawn public transportation that were becoming increasingly available. In cities and towns, hackney coaches and sedan chairs were available for hire, and some stage lines were developed for overland travel between populated areas.

The nineteenth century saw further expansion and improvement of roads in Europe and the United States, which led to many changes in the design, production and use of horse-drawn vehicles. A major road surface improvement, for example, was macadam, a road pavement with a bituminous or crushed-rock binder that was introduced in England in 1815 by John McAdam. During this period a variety of vehicles was used, from simple owner-driven carts to very formal coachman-driven carriages accompanied by grooms and footmen.

In America, particularly, improvements in technology and production methods during the second half of the century resulted in the manufacture of modestly-priced vehicles in large quantity. At long last, many members of the American middle class could afford to own and drive their own vehicles. The wealthy, however, turned to increasingly specialized and sometimes custom-made vehicles for various purposes, such as sport and pleasure driving.

Public transportation also expanded significantly and became more diversified, with the development of cabs, omnibuses and horse trolleys in cities and the proliferation of stage lines in rural areas.

In the early twentieth century the automobile gained popularity and rapidly replaced horse-drawn vehicles, especially for personal transportation. Working vehicles like the trade wagons that delivered ice, milk, groceries and farm produce continued in use until the 1920s and 1930s, when they, too, were replaced by gasoline-powered trucks. Although the Carriage Era came to an end, limited sport and recreational driving continued in Europe and the United States into the automotive age. Encouraged by the Carriage Association of America, founded in 1960, and the American Driving Society, founded in 1971, pleasure driving experienced a significant revival. These organizations have sponsored meets and informal competitions throughout the United States and have contributed to a renewed and growing interest in pleasure driving.

EUROPEAN VEHICLES

In Europe, horse-drawn vehicles were rarely used for transporting passengers until the sixteenth century. First used only by royalty, early vehicles such as coaches and sleighs rapidly gained popularity with members of the aristocracy. Standard reference sources concur that the coach, an enclosed, four-wheel vehicle often used with four horses, was probably invented in Hungary in the mid-fifteenth century and that its name derives from Kocz, the town of its origin. Many of these vehicles were elaborately decorated so as to display the wealth and social status of their owners. As was typical with the decorative arts of this period, the functional elements of these vehicles were obscured by lavish embellishments, paintings, carvings and gold leaf. Recreational sleighs used by royalty or the wealthy were often carved and fancifully decorated to resemble unicorns, dragons, lions or allegorical forms.

By the end of the seventeenth century a number of technical innovations had been introduced to improve the comfort and durability of vehicles, among them the use of metal leaf springs and the double perch. The Worshipful Company of Coach and Harness Makers of London was established in 1677—much later than guilds in other trades, which were common in England by the fifteenth century. The need for such a regulatory fraternity to control the quality of work and the monopoly of the trade in that city may well indicate a significant increase in carriage production by the second half of the seventeenth century.

Improvements in construction and new designs flourished at the end of the eighteenth century in Europe and led to the development of such popular and basic types of vehicles as the landau, the barouche, the curricle, the post-chaise, the sociable and the many types of phaetons. The C-spring was introduced in 1800 and elliptic springs, destined to be the most widely-used suspension system during the Carriage Era, were introduced shortly thereafter. Improvements in vehicles and concurrent improvements in roads in many parts of Europe increased both the popularity of and the demand for carriages. Some forms of public transportation were also available, among them the hackney coach and sedan chair.

Although many new carriage designs were developed by coach builders, others were contributed in the early nineteenth century by inventive members of the aristocracy who submitted their designs to preeminent carriage building firms. Among them were the Count d'Orsay of France and Lord Clarence and Lord Peter Henry Brougham of England, whose designs produced popular vehicles that still carry their names. Designs from one country were freely adapted by coach builders in other parts of Europe and in the United States. The Germans were known for the landau and the barouche, the French for the caleche and for superb finishes and lavish interior trimming and the English for the mail coach, the posting chariot and a high quality of construction. The American carriage-building tradition, initially grounded in European and especially English design, became known for lighter construction.

The European vehicles presented here range from an Italian gig dated 1670, the oldest vehicle in The Museums collection, to the 1850 state coach of Prince Adelbert of Bavaria, one of four Wittelsbach state vehicles in The Museums Collection.

Before Bohemian Ann was Queen,
Astride their steeds were ladies seen;
And Good Queen Bess to Paul's, I wot,
Full oft astride hers jogg'd on Trot;
Beaus then could foot it thro' all weather,
And nothing feared but wear of leather.
But now (as luxury decrees)
The polish'd age rolls on at ease:
Coach, chariot, chaise, berlin, landau
(Machines the ancients never saw)
Indulge our gentle sons of war,
Who ne'er will mount triumphant car.
The carriage marks the peer's degree,
And almost tells the doctor's fee;
Bears ever thriving child of art;
Ev'n thieves to Tyburn claim their cart.

Sylvanus Urban in *The Gentleman's Magazine,*
(London: E. Cane, February, 1747) 94.

**Promenade au Bois de Boulogne—Attelage a la
Daumont *1860; Louis-Emanuel Soulange-Teissier,
lithographer; Goupil & Co., publisher; Paris, France;
Museums collection***

1. Gig

Maker unknown, Italy; c. 1670
164 × 66 × 57 in (417 × 168 × 145 cm)
Exterior, interior original; Gift of Ward
Melville, 1971

This gig, which can also be called a chaise, is the oldest vehicle in The Museums collection and is an excellent example of the attention carriage makers of the period gave to ornamentation. This vehicle would not have provided a comfortable ride, since the seat is mounted directly onto the long, straight shafts. The step iron is placed on the shaft well in front of the seat. The seat pillars are splayed and carved with a tulip design and scrolled ends. The exterior is painted red and green. Painted decoration includes an angular orange line a half inch wide framing a cluster of flowers on the back and sides of the seat. The corners of the seat riser are edged in a painted ribbon motif. A swag and tassel crest adorns the front of the seat riser, below which is an undecipherable Italian inscription. The floor of the toeboard is decorated with painted white tulips, a motif repeated in various sizes throughout the vehicle.

The interior of the seat is painted in mottled browns and golds. The seat is covered with a small cushion of rose silk shot with silver thread and edged with silver fringe.

The crossbar and swingletree are carved and painted. A footman's standard hangs from leather straps off the axle. The high wheels are extensively and delicately painted with fine lines and abstract geometric patterns. The hub bands are flanged brass and the tire irons are studded.

Rear of the gig, showing decorative painting

2. Sleigh

Maker unknown, France; c. 1780
90 × 42 × 32 in (229 × 107 × 81 cm)
Exterior, interior original; Gift of James
Keillor, 1952

Many European sleighs were designed for a single passenger and a driver. The driver sat astride a seat at the rear and could control the sideways slip of the sleigh with his feet or with spikes that were sometimes attached to the footplates. The reins passed on either side of the passenger. These fanciful and sometimes flamboyant sleighs must have presented an extraordinary sight as they were driven over snow-covered paths or frozen rivers and lakes. They were sometimes used at night with torchlight to illuminate the path.

This sleigh is carved and hollowed from a single piece of wood with additional jointed sections. The mane and clenched paws of the lion are naturalistically carved.

The lion's face is enlivened by wide eyes, flared nostrils and a gaping mouth, and its tongue is extended and loosely jointed.

Between the paint layer and the wood there is a layer of gesso, which conceals the grain of the wood. The body is painted a brownish yellow; the upper rim shows traces of gold leaf.

The driver's seat, above the lion's tail, is trimmed in red velvet and blue gimp shot with silver thread. The interior has no trim extant.

The carved and painted runners and knees are red accented with gilt striping. Iron footplates, bolted to the runner ends, are provided for the driver's feet.

3. Berlin Coach

Maker unknown, France; c. 1780
192 × 88 × 75 in (488 × 224 × 191 cm)
Exterior original; interior trim and
hammercloth restored prior to 1953
Museums purchase, 1953

The berlin coach was invented circa 1660 by Col. Philip de Chiese, an Italian employed by the King of Prussia. It was named after that country's capital city. The berlin represented a major innovation in the design of coach undercarriage construction: to reduce the weight of the vehicle and improve its balance, two lighter perches instead of a single heavy perch were used to connect the front transom to the rear axle. The curved "crane-neck" perches used in this vehicle allow the front wheels to turn under the body, decreasing the turning radius needed by the vehicle; earlier forms of the berlin featured straight double perches. Whip springs, used in conjunction with leather braces, decreased the swinging motion associated with earlier coaches that had braces connected to rigid pillars.

Although the berlin undercarriage design is usually associated with coach construction, it was also used with other types of vehicles.

The entire body of the coach is gilded wood. The panels are decorated with painted allegorical figures bordered by floral and fruit clusters. The band below the windows has a border of eagles and lions. Carved and gilded figures are attached to the corner pillars of the body. The hammercloth is of red striped voided velvet.

The ormolu door handles and the brace buckles are cast with a decorative banding in a tulip motif. The material and design of this hardware are repeated in the harness for this berlin, which is also in The Museums collection.

This coach was sent from France to Rome in 1785 as a gift to the Marchioness Pianetti and was later used by Cardinal Pianetti, a high prelate of the Pontifical Court.

4. State Coach

M. Staubwasser, Munich, Germany; c. 1850
148 × 84 × 74 in (376 × 213 × 188 cm)
Exterior, interior original; Gift of Dieter
Holterbosch, 1967

The state coach was a formal vehicle used by royalty or high officials in processions and on state business. Unlike the state coaches of previous centuries which were covered with lavish decoration, nineteenth-century coaches were simplified and understated in appearance, in accordance with prevailing tastes. Improved technology in coach-building also increased their comfort.

The body is painted blue with black upper quarter panels and is decorated with the Wittelsbach coat of arms painted on the door panels. Crowns are painted on the side panels and the doors and in front of the toeboard. The pump handles, the footman's cushion standard, the boot supports and the ends of the springs terminate in carved and gilded leaf decoration. The silver and gilt door handles also carry the Wittelsbach coat of arms. The off-white wool hammercloth has light yellow silk fringe and twisted silver thread rosettes and carries an enamelled Wittelsbach coat of arms on either side.

The interior is trimmed in off-white brocades in various patterns and the floor is covered with an off-white carpet. Rose silk

Interior of the state coach

satin curtains can be drawn at the windows for privacy. All the interior fittings, such as the pulleys for the coachman's check-string, or signal cord, are of carved ivory. The vehicle is suspended on C-springs and under springs.

This state coach is one of four vehicles in The Museums collection that belonged to Prince Adelbert of Bavaria (1818–1875), the youngest son of King Ludwig I of the Wittelsbach Dynasty (see Cat. No. 5). The family used this vehicle until the monarchy was overthrown in 1918.

5. Grand Duc

F. D. Gmelch, Munich, Germany; c. 1850
149 × 84 × 72 in (378 × 213 × 183 cm)
Exterior, interior original; Gift of Dieter Holterbosch, 1966

A number of nineteenth-century vehicles like this grand duc, also called a *hof wagen*, were designed so the passengers could be seen by pedestrians or by passengers in other carriages. These types of vehicles were popular with women who exhibited their most elegant dress as they were driven in city parks such as Central Park in New York City, Hyde Park in London and the Bois de Boulogne in Paris. The grand duc was a formal vehicle and generally driven postilion, with the near-side horse—the horse closest to the vehicle on the driver's left—being ridden and guided by the rider, instead of being driven by a coachman on the carriage.

The profile of this vehicle resembles an elongated nautilus shell. It is hung low to the ground for easy access, and the interior area, though quite shallow, is spacious. Low folding steps are provided on both sides. The ease of accessibility and the spacious interior accommodated the voluminous skirts that were the fashion for women in the mid-nineteenth century. The lack of side panels permitted a clear view of the passengers from the outside.

The body is painted blue and the hardware is silver-plated. The wide and slanted dash has a lamp socket mounted on each side. The vehicle has a boot in front for luggage and a footman's seat at the rear where the hand brake is engaged. The Wittelsbach coat of arms is painted on both sides.

The interior trim is an off-white silk and linen brocade in a crown pattern and all interior fittings are of carved ivory. The vehicle is hung on elliptic and C-springs.

This duc is one of four vehicles in The Museums collection that belonged to Prince Adelbert of Bavaria.

6. Britzka

*Beaumont & Taylor, London, England
c. 1820; 141 × 95 × 68 in
(358 × 241 × 172 cm); Exterior restored
prior to 1962; interior original; Museums
purchase, 1962*

The britzka, a vehicle of Austrian design, was introduced in England in 1818 by the English coach builder T. G. Adams. It gained popularity as a convenient long-distance traveling carriage because the interior could be converted to a sleeping compartment and the body had ample space for luggage. It was used extensively in Europe until railroad service became available. With the forward seats folded down, the carriage accommodated two passengers. With the seat raised, four passengers could sit facing each other. During long, overnight journeys, passengers could lie full length inside the vehicle, protected by the closed wooden shutter and the extended leather knee apron.

The body has a folding top, folding glass shutters to protect passengers from inclement weather and folding steps on the exterior to conserve interior space. The boots under the driver's seat and the groom's seat at the rear carried luggage. A sword case at the rear of the vehicle held swords and firearms and could be reached from the interior by the removal of the interior "squab," an upholstered backrest. The body is painted green and decorated with black striping. An unidentified crest is painted on each door and the door handles are silver-plated.

The interior and hood lining are trimmed in white wool and white broadlace, as are the driver's and groom's seats.

The britzka is suspended on C-springs. Attached to the heavy perch by a chain is a skid, a manually applied chock to slow or stop the vehicle during steep descents.

PERSONAL TRANSPORTATION
In Pre-Industrial America

In pre-industrial America, privately owned vehicles used for personal transportation rather than for work were classified as "pleasure vehicles." The earliest vehicles in America were undoubtedly designed not for pleasure but for work—simply-made carts, wagons and sleds crafted by carpenters, wheelwrights and perhaps even farmers. In the last part of the seventeenth century, wealthy men in the colonies—such as governors, successful merchants and owners of large farms and plantations—imported carriages from Europe for personal transportation. The earliest of these were probably the coach and the smaller and lighter chariot, no examples of which are in The Museums collection.

In the seventeenth and eighteenth centuries several different styles of small, open carriages were imported or domestically manufactured. Among them were the two-wheel chaise, which featured a folding hood, and open two-wheel vehicles such as the chair, whiskey and gig. The names of some of these vehicles were used interchangeably in accounts of the period. By the early nineteenth century American adaptations of the coach and the chariot, called coachee and chariotee, were introduced.

Carriage making was a complex undertaking requiring the labor of craftsmen with specialized skills—woodworkers, wheelwrights, blacksmiths, upholsterers, painters, stripers and varnishers—and a considerable investment of capital for materials and labor. American carriage manufacturing began during the mid-eighteenth century in urban centers such as Boston, New York and Philadelphia. The first carriage makers were immigrants who had learned the trade in European carriage shops, and the vehicles they produced were based on European designs. The American Revolutionary War diminished the production of luxuries in America, including carriages; after the war, the new nation embarked on an era of economic expansion, and carriage makers, as well as other manufacturers, were encouraged by protective legislation and favorable tariffs.

American Friends Going to Meeting in Summer *1811; from* Travels in Some parts of North America in the Years 1804, 1805, and 1806; *Robert Sutcliff, author; C. Peacock, publisher; York, London, England; Photograph Courtesy of The New-York Historical Society, New York City*

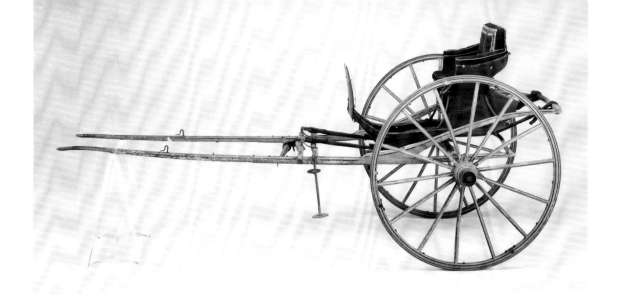

Pleasure vehicles remained expensive to purchase and to maintain. The well-to-do had a number of vehicles in their stables, while the less affluent aspired to own a single vehicle. The majority of Americans in the decades after the Revolutionary War still continued to travel by water, on foot, on horseback or in stagecoaches that were available for public transportation in the more settled regions along the eastern coast.

Geographic factors as well as personal wealth dictated the distribution of privately-owned vehicles in America. In commercially developed cities and towns and their surrounding areas, there were many more vehicles per capita than in sparsely populated frontier settlements and more recently established towns, where vehicles for farming and freight hauling were more essential for survival than luxuries such as pleasure vehicles.

One of the first vehicle styles developed in America was the pleasure wagon, produced in New England at the beginning of the nineteenth century. It combined the functions of a work vehicle with those of a passenger vehicle because it had easily removable seats. The vehicle that evolved from the early-nineteenth-century pleasure wagon was the American buggy, which became, in its many varied styles, the most popular vehicle on American roads by the end of the nineteenth century. The vehicles in this section are arranged chronologically and include vehicles such as the gig, the chaise, the basket wagon, the pleasure wagon and the hooded buggy.

7. Gig

Maker unknown, United States; 1760–1780
155 × 62 × 72 in (394 × 157 × 183 cm)
Exterior, interior original; Gift of the
Society of the Cincinnati of the State of
New Hampshire, 1953

This eighteenth-century gig is a sophisticated riding chair. It has a boot at the rear of the seat. The seat is painted black and has an ogee back with scroll terminations.

The seat, trimmed in blue wool edged with blue, red and white broadlace and narrow seaming lace, has a square back and padded armrests. The dash is leather. The floor has a black painted carpet with a stenciled white cross pattern edged in a white Greek key pattern border. The boot knob and the dash rail are silver-plated.

The gig is suspended on thoroughbraces. These are mounted on a fluted, curved and bent transom, which is mounted in turn on cantilevered wood supports. The step plate, used to enter the vehicle, is mounted well in front of the body. The turned axles are of wood. The gear, or undercarriage, is painted bright yellow with black stripes.

This vehicle originally belonged to the Brinckerhoff family of Chittanango in Madison County, New York.

8. Chaise

Maker unknown, United States; c. 1810
155 × 85 × 75 in (394 × 216 × 191 cm)
Exterior, interior original; Gift of Elizabeth
L. Godwin, 1951

The term *chaise*, from the French word for chair, was applied to these popular, two-wheel vehicles drawn by one horse. Used during the eighteenth and nineteenth centuries in the United States, the vehicle was sometimes called a "shay," an American

derivation from the French *chaise*. This example is a later variant of the 1700s gig (see Cat. No. 7). It is typical of those produced and used in New England.

This chaise has a folding leather hood with a large oval light, or window, at either side and in the back. The body, relatively shallow, has ogee side panels and is painted black with red and yellow striping.

The interior trim is blue wool, edged in figured broadlace. The floor is covered with a black painted carpet with red and white stenciling.

This chaise has elongated wooden shafts that form cantilevered springs. The undercarriage has leather thoroughbraces hung from the rear crossbar and used in conjunction with the shafts.

9. Four-Wheel Chaise

Maker unknown, United States or France
c. 1780; 121 × 90 × 68 in
(307 × 228 × 173 cm); Exterior original;
head leather, interior trim conserved 1984
Gift of the Johnstown Historical Society,
Johnstown, New York, 1955

This chaise is an excellent example of fine pre-industrial craftsmanship. The curved back terminates in a scroll motif, and the vehicle has a folding leather hood mounted on wooden bows and sockets. Leather budgets, or boots, are located at both the front and rear. The single perch is chamfered and painted dark yellow with broad black striping.

The body is painted dark green and features family emblems at the footboard, back and sides. The interior is trimmed in white wool and white brocade broadlace. The floor is covered with a painted carpet and a woven floor carpet that has a floral motif enclosed in squares. The body is mounted on whip springs and the pump handles are finished with scrolled, carved rosettes. The folding steps slide under the body on an iron track. The axles are also dark yellow with the same broad black striping as the perch.

This chaise is believed to have been owned by the American Revolutionary War hero General Peter Gansevoort of Albany, New York. Gansevoort family tradition relates that the vehicle was imported from France. The wood used in the vehicle, however, appears to be of North American origin, providing some evidence that the chaise may have been made in the United States. General Gansevoort's granddaughter, Mrs. Gansevoort Lansing, gave the chaise to the nineteenth-century American genre artist Edward Lamson Henry. The artist, who is noted for his detailed depictions of early American life, featured this vehicle in numerous paintings, including *One Hundred Years Ago* (1887), *Waiting for the Ferry* (1899) and *Passing the Outposts* (1903).

10. Basket Wagon

*Maker unknown, probably United States
c. 1810; 127 × 105 × 69 in
(323 × 267 × 175 cm); Exterior, interior
original; draperies conserved 1985; Gift of
William Jarvis, Jr., in memory of
Lucretia Jarvis, 1957*

The body of this basket wagon is made of yellow-painted willow. The curved canvas-covered top, supported by slender wooden pillars, is lined with a patterned blue silk. The branched steps are made of wrought iron; the handles, dash rail, loops and nuts are silver-plated.

The seat and fall curtain are trimmed in red velvet, edged with a two-inch needle-point border in a Greek key pattern. A red and yellow patterned silk and linen decorative drapery, edged in twisted silk fringe, is attached to the lower edge of the top. Made of a continuous piece of fabric, the shallow drapery was drawn up into swags by leather strips. Beige linsey-woolsey roll-up curtains, originally lined with blue silk, are fitted at the sides and rear of the body.

The wagon belonged to the United States diplomat Dr. Leonard Jarvis, of Claremont, New Hampshire. According to an 1895 book, *History of the Town of Claremont, New Hampshire*, by Otis F. R. Waite, General Lafayette of France rode in this carriage during his celebrated tour of the United States in 1825. The general, after visiting the New Hampshire legislature in session in Concord, traveled to the towns of Bradford, Newport and Claremont, where he spent the night. The following morning, June 27, 1825, Dr. Jarvis drove the general in this carriage to Windsor, Vermont, some ten miles northwest of Claremont, across the Connecticut River.[1]

[1]Otis F. R. Waite, *History of the Town of Claremont, New Hampshire* (Manchester, New Hampshire: Clarke, 1895) 380.

11. Pleasure Wagon

Maker unknown, United States; c. 1820
99 × 91 × 68 in (251 × 231 × 173 cm)
Exterior, interior original; Gift of the
Johnstown Historical Society, Johnstown,
New York, 1955

The pleasure wagon is a vehicle type developed in New England during the first quarter of the nineteenth century, often constructed with removable seats to convert it from a passenger to a freight wagon.

The ribbed body is boat-shaped, to prevent cargo from shifting outward or back and slipping out of the vehicle. The body has an ogee back and scrolled terminations at the cross members of the panels. It is painted light green with broad yellow and black striping that accentuates its ribbed construction. A cherub is painted on the rear panel. The railing around the body is covered in braided leather. The canvas top is painted to make it waterproof.

The interior trim is leather edged in pasting lace and broadlace. The pleasure wagon is suspended on elliptic springs (these springs are mounted parallel to the axles, an arrangement referred to as "end springs") and the hardware is hand-forged.

This vehicle was acquired by the American artist Edward Lamson Henry during the nineteenth century. He featured the wagon in his painting *The Watering Trough* (1900), which is also in The Museums collection.

12. Pleasure Wagon

Maker unknown, United States; c. 1820
114 × 68 × 72 in (290 × 173 × 183 cm)
Exterior, interior original; Museums
purchase, 1952

The body of this pleasure wagon is curved or swelled, with raved, or ribbed, sides. The broad black decorative striping applied over the yellow ochre paint gives the appearance of paneling. The cross members of the body and spring block have carved scroll terminations. The wagon has two seats mounted on double wooden cantilevered members. The seat rails are curved, with scrolled ends, and have splayed and turned spindle supports on the sides and back. The front seat back can be folded forward for access to the rear seat. The spindles are decorated with black stenciled leaves outlined with a fine yellow stripe. The original folding top is missing.

The seats have padded armrests and the remaining fragments of trim are of brown leather edged in red, black and yellow seaming lace.

The axle and reach are chamfered; the double- and singletrees are turned. The pleasure wagon is suspended on elliptic springs. All of the hardware is hand-forged. The wheels are secured by linchpins. The gear is also painted yellow ochre and extensively striped in black. The initials "OM" or "DM" carved under the floorboards are presumed to be those of the carriage maker.

13. Hooded Buggy

Maker unknown, United States; c. 1830
94 × 84 × 74 in (239 × 213 × 188 cm)
Exterior, interior original; hood possibly restored prior to 1962; Gift of Webster Knight II, 1962

This hooded buggy is an early, rural predecessor of the mass-produced buggies of the late nineteenth century. In comparison with later buggies (see Cat. Nos. 14 and 15) this buggy is heavier: it has entirely hand-hewn wooden members, thicker hubs and spokes and considerably wider axles. The ratio between the diameters of the front and rear wheels is also greater and the suspension system is more primitive than those of later buggies.

The shallow body, painted black with red striping, supports a high folding hood of painted canvas. The seat has a narrow lazy back, or cushion, trimmed in cream-colored wool with red tufts. The padded armrests are edged with red and green pasting lace and the fall curtain is trimmed with particularly fine broadlace in an entwined leaf pattern in red and green.

The buggy is hung on thoroughbraces. The rigidity of the undercarriage necessitated the use of a snipebill, a crude substitute for a kingpin, to hold the plates of the bolster and axle together. This arrangement was rather unstable and caused the front axle to rock back and forth when stationary. This flexibility of the axle and bolster allowed the shafts to rest on the ground when not in use; exertion from the horse in draft pulled the members flush.[1]

---

[1] In later carriages, when steam-bending of wood became a common practice, the heels or ends that attached directly to the carriage were curved. The shaft couplings, which attached the shafts to the axle, were made with a sufficient amount of play, or space, in the hardware to allow the shafts to be lowered or raised with relative ease.

PERSONAL TRANSPORTATION
In Industrial America

During the second half of the nineteenth century, significant technological and organizational developments in American manufacturing contributed to major changes in the patterns of ownership and use of horse-drawn vehicles. The "American System of Manufactures,"[1] characterized by the use of power machinery, the standardization and interchangeability of parts and the subdivision of labor, substantially reduced production costs and made horse-drawn carriages affordable to more people.

Many vehicles were now produced in large factories and shipped to sales rooms, called repositories, in major American cities. The Studebaker Brothers Manufacturing Company of South Bend, Indiana, for example, occupied a 26-acre site by 1876; in 1872 they advertised that they produced one vehicle every seven minutes.[2] By the end of the century, Studebaker had repositories in New York, Chicago, Kansas City, Denver, Salt Lake City, San Francisco, Portland, Oregon, and St. Joseph, Missouri.[3] Some dealers carried new vehicles from a variety of manufacturers as well as second-hand vehicles for sale. In 1900 a reported 907,482 vehicles for personal transportation, for work and for pleasure were produced by American carriage manufacturers.[4]

By the late nineteenth century the most popular vehicle in America was the typical buggy, a light, four-wheel carriage with or without a collapsible top and accommodating one or two persons. By the beginning of the twentieth century mass production had lowered costs so substantially that mail-order catalogs advertised simple vehicles for as little as twenty dollars apiece. In 1900 the average annual earnings of a non-farm employee were $483 and steak cost 13.2 cents per pound.[5]

Some widely-used vehicles in America were surreys, four-wheel family carriages built in a variety of styles, usually with a top; road carts, light two-wheel carts built for one or two passengers; and versatile family wagons that could be converted from passenger to freight vehicles by the removal of seats. At the more elegant end of the spectrum of mass-produced vehicles were the rockaways, enclosed vehicles that could be driven by the owner or a coachman.

The buggies, wagons, trap and rockaways shown here are arranged from the simplest and least expensive to the more elegant and costly. They represent the major types of carriages used for personal transportation by individuals and families during the last decades of the nineteenth century and the first decades of the twentieth. These types of vehicles were among the first to be displaced by automobiles, especially by the Model T introduced by Henry Ford in 1908. The Model T was produced by an efficient assembly line, adapted and improved from the "American System of Manufactures" that had revolutionized the horse-drawn vehicle industry some fifty years earlier. Some styles of buggies are not included here, among them the piano box buggy and the corning buggy.

Coming from the Trot *1873; Haskell and Allen,
publisher; Boston, Massachusetts; Museums collection*

[1]Anonymous, "Subdivision of Labor in Carriage-Building," *The Hub* (Vol. 17, No. 4, July 1875) 122, and Nathan
Rosenberg, ed., *The American System of Manufactures
(1854–1855)* (Edinburgh: Edinburgh University Press, 1969)
1–86.

[2]Advertising poster for Studebaker, 1872, illustrated in
Edwin Corle, *John Studebaker, An American Dream* (New York,
E. P. Dutton & Co., Inc., 1948).

[3]Studebaker Bros. Mfg. Co., *Fine Carriages, Buggies,
Passenger Wagons*, Catalogue No. 97 (January 1, 1897).

[4]James K. Davies, "Carriages and Wagons," in *Census
Reports, Volume X, Twelfth Census of the United States, Taken in the
Year 1900. Manufactures, Part IV—Special Reports on Selected
Industries* (Washington, D.C.: United States Printing Office,
1902) 305.

[5]*Historical Statistics of the United States: Colonial Times to
1970* (Washington, D.C.: Bureau of the Census, 1976) 165,
213.

14. Stanhope Buggy

*Studebaker Brothers Manufacturing
Company, South Bend, Indiana; c. 1910
95 × 95 × 62 in (241 × 241 × 157 cm)
Exterior, interior original; seat restored 1981
Gift of Joyce Barber, 1969*

The term *stanhope* was first applied to a type of English gig invented by Fitzroy Stanhope during the early nineteenth century. This buggy resembles that earlier vehicle only in the curved lines of the front seat panels, or risers, known as "stanhope pillars."

The body is painted black and has red striping. The leather folding top is lined in blue wool. Leather or canvas storm curtains, not included with this example, could be attached to the sides. The large, comfortable seat is trimmed in heavy blue wool. A storage compartment beneath the seat is accessible through a hinged door beneath the seat cushion. The buggy is suspended on elliptic springs and the wheels are fitted with rubber tires.[1]

This model was called the " 'Izzer' Stanhope" in the 1913 Studebaker catalog. The name was a clever adaptation of rural colloquialisms: "izzer" meant something that is, in the present, as opposed to a "wuzzer," something that was, in the past. The company used the name to distinguish its product from those of competitors. Along with the piano-box buggy, not shown here, this vehicle became one of the most popular buggies in the United States.

[1]Rubber tires were first used on carriages in England in the 1870s; by 1895 their use was widespread in Europe and the United States.

15. Doctor's Buggy

*Fouts & Hunter Carriage Manufacturing
Company, Terre Haute, Indiana; c. 1911
103 × 84 × 65 in (262 × 213 × 165 cm)
Exterior, interior original; Gift of Ward
Melville, 1971*

The Fouts & Hunter Company manufactured a line of durable and reasonably-
priced buggies, designated "Life Savers for
Land Travellers" in one of their undated
late-nineteenth-century catalogs in The
Museums Carriage Reference Library. The
advertising promised that, in addition to
providing comfort at low cost, this vehicle
"keeps you in better humor and prolongs
your life." It was well-suited for doctors who
might encounter all sorts of weather and
road conditions.

The body features roll-back side
curtains to shelter the driver from rain, snow
or dust. For fair-weather travel, the patented
storm-proof top, windshield and side
curtains could easily be removed to convert
the buggy to an open vehicle. The body is
painted black. The leather top is lined and
the seat is trimmed in leather. The buggy is
suspended on elliptic springs. Patent information is marked on a brass plate: "Jan.
16.06.—No. 810151/Sept. 11.06—No.
830664/April 19.10—No. 955404/Dec.
13.10—No. 13183/Feb. 7.11—No. 983371/
May 9.11—No. 13235."

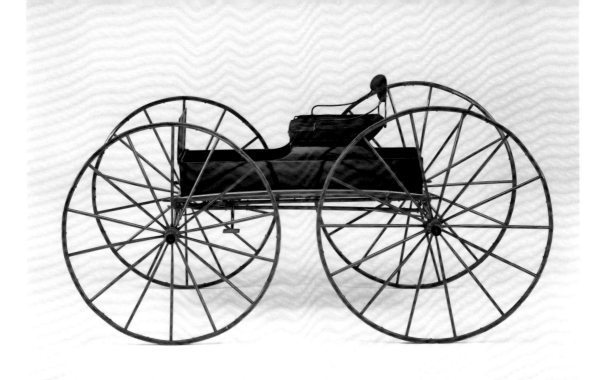

16. Road Wagon

John Curley, Brooklyn, New York; c. 1880
99 × 52 × 47 in (251 × 132 × 119 cm)
Exterior restored 1954; interior original,
with seat restored 1954; Museums purchase,
1953

During the late nineteenth century, light, fast vehicles were developed in response to the country's fascination with speed and the popularity of racing trotters hitched to lightweight vehicles. Lithographs of the period depict main thoroughfares crowded with road wagons and other light vehicles, their drivers vying for the lead in impromptu races. Though similar to a buggy in form, the road wagon is much simplified, being essentially a box on extremely thin-spoked wheels. The reduction in weight made it light, suited for speed and very affordable.

This road wagon has a narrow, unornamented piano box body. It has side-bar springs, a type patented by J. B. Brewster of New York. The felloes and the spokes are only one-half inch in diameter.

John Curley began his carriage business in 1867. By 1880, his shop produced a variety of vehicles, including phaetons, village carts, vis-a-vis and cabriolets. The manufacturer's serial number, marked on the seat, is 796.

17. Skeleton Wagon
Maker unknown, United States; c. 1860
100 × 64 × 49 in (254 × 163 × 124 cm)
Restored 1954; Museums purchase, 1953

This wagon is a typical example of the extremely lightweight vehicles that were developed for trotting races in the second half of the nineteenth century. The frame, merely a skeleton of heavier road wagons, shows a masterful reduction of a vehicle to its essential functioning parts.

The caned seat mounted on the skeleton frame has a shallow iron railing at the sides and back. The entire vehicle is painted off-white with red striping. The light, equirotal wheels, of equal diameter, have spokes and felloes less than one-half inch in diameter to reduce even further the exertion required for a fast-paced trotter to pull the wagon in races.

18. Democrat Wagon

G. W. Farrar & Sons, Peterboro, New Hampshire; c. 1895; 100 × 65 × 60 in (254 × 165 × 152 cm); Exterior, interior original; Gift of The Society for the Preservation of New England Antiquities, Boston, Massachusetts, 1951

Though the exact derivation of the name *democrat wagon* is unknown, tradition attributes it to the unassuming and unostentatious appearance of the vehicle, symbolizing the equality of man.

The body is of natural, varnished wood. The seat rails are curved and have turned spindle supports. The sides and rear are paneled. The seat risers—wooden panels supporting the seats—have oval cut-outs, contributing to the graceful, light appearance of this modest and affordable vehicle. The two seats can be removed to convert the vehicle for carrying cargo.

The hardware and felloes are painted a light ochre, accented in red striping. The floor covering is painted canvas with a black-and-white pattern. The seat trim is a dark brown leather.

The vehicle has a foot brake and is suspended with a "Concord" gear, an arrangement of half elliptic springs mounted at right angles to the axle on either side and with three reaches connecting the axles. The drop-axles allow the body to be mounted lower to the ground for easy access.

19. Platform Wagon

Coles, Baldwin & Bentley, Port Jefferson, New York; c. 1900 121 × 72 × 65 in (307 × 183 × 165 cm) Exterior restored after 1951; interior original Museums purchase, 1951

The platform wagon was designed as a multi-purpose family vehicle in rural areas for those who could afford only a single carriage. With the seats in place, it was a passenger-carrying vehicle for trips to church and visits to neighbors. With the rear two seats removed, it was transformed into a work vehicle for transporting goods to and from town.

This wagon has a simple box body and a plain wooden dash. The seat cushions are made of painted canvas, a less expensive material than leather. Sturdy platform springs, a combination of cross and side springs, were used to accommodate a variety of loads.

The company that manufactured this vehicle was probably established in the 1870s, for it does not appear in the 1870 United States Census reports. If it existed before that date, its value of goods accumulated did not exceed the $500 minimum for that year's manufacturing report. A newspaper advertisement in the June 19, 1875, *Long Island Leader* reports that the company built both heavy and light carriages, as well as hearses as "a specialty," and that it also did repairs and upholstery work. The 1880 *Products of Industry Report, U.S. Census,* indicates that Coles, Baldwin & Bentley had eight employees at a time when most rural manufacturers had two, and that the value of their products, sold and unsold, totalled $6,000. The level of their investment in labor and goods places them among the largest carriage manufacturers on Long Island during the period, surpassed only by Downs of Huntington and Blydenburgh of Riverhead.

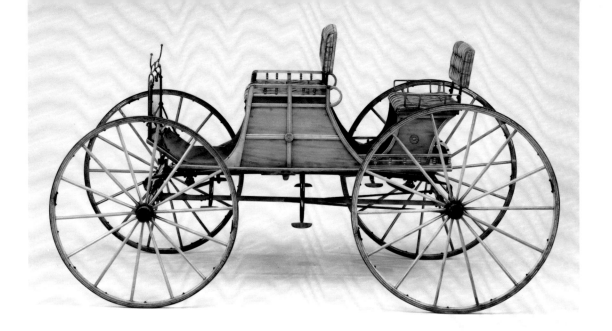

20. Trap

Troy Carriage Works, Troy, New York; c. 1895
113 × 64 × 60 in (287 × 163 × 152 cm)
Exterior, interior restored 1953; Gift of
Katherine Thayer Hobson, 1953

The term *trap* was applied originally to all forms of light pleasure vehicles. In the late nineteenth century in America, the term came to be used to describe vehicles with shifting, sliding or collapsible seats to accommodate more passengers without increasing the length of the vehicle or altering the arrangement of the seats. Hundreds of patents were issued for the mechanisms for such seats, and the vehicle was extremely popular by the last decades of the Carriage Era. A government survey in 1899 shows that only 15 fewer traps were made than the combined number of victorias, cabriolets, vis-a-vis, broughams, clarences and landaus produced in that year. The Troy Carriage Works patented this vehicle type in 1891.

This example, which was also called a "jump-seat buckboard," has paneled sides finished in varnished natural wood. Its two-seat arrangement could be converted to a single seat, leaving a shallow open storage area surrounded by a turned spindle side rail, by collapsing the rear hinged lazy back and brass arm rails, tilting the front seat forward and folding the entire rear seat under the front seat. The leather seat cushions are painted a light brown.

The body is set on side springs on the front bolster and the rear dropped axle. This crank-shaped axle permitted the body to be hung lower to the ground for easy access. A wooden reach connects the axles. It has simple step irons on each side and the entire undercarriage is accented with red striping.

The trap with a single seat in front, the rear seat having been folded under the front seat.

21. Rockaway

Studebaker Brothers Manufacturing Company, South Bend, Indiana; c. 1885
120 × 86 × 65 in (305 × 218 × 165 cm)
Exterior, interior original; Gift of F. M. Kirby, 1956

The rockaway was a distinctly American vehicle type developed in the 1830s by a carriage maker in Jamaica, New York. Its name, derived from an adjacent town, was used to distinguish this manufacturer's vehicle from those of his competitors. The design evolved from the early vernacular coachee and germantown, which had a roof supported by fixed pillars. Rockaways were later developed in a profusion of styles that resembled broughams, station wagons and enclosed coaches, and were extremely popular to the end of the Carriage Era.

This example of a rockaway has a cut-under body and open sides and is painted black. A small monogram, either "GW" or "GWC," appears in shaded blue letters on the door panels. The side curtains of leather are lined in blue wool. The seats are trimmed in russet-colored leather.

The body is suspended on elliptic springs. The reach is fitted with roller rub irons to prevent the rubber-tired wheels from binding. The quick-release shackles for the shaft indicate that the vehicle could be used with either a single horse or a pair.

Manufacturer's tags on the rear and on the hub nuts read "Studebaker/New York," indicating that the vehicle was sold through the company's respository in New York City. Another tag under the driver's seat describes the quality and range of Studebaker's products. The brakes have a raised inscription, "BR/BL, Potter's, Pat. Oct. 18, Dec. 27 '87, Apr. 5 '82." The first letters indicate brake right/brake left.

22. Coupé Rockaway

A. S. Flandrau, New York, New York; 1871
120 × 88 × 68 in (304 × 224 × 173 cm)
Exterior, interior original; Gift of Franklin
Joseph, 1962

This rockaway is a superb example of design and use of materials in an otherwise popular vehicle type. Each section of the body combines to create a pleasing and continuous line and its interior trim reflects the work that could be specified by a customer. Like all rockaways, it could be coachman- or owner-driven.

The panel body is painted black, accented with gold striping. The lower rear quarter panels terminate in an ogee shape.

The partition separating the driver's and passengers' seats has a sliding glass above the trimmed back; this shifting front can be removed and replaced with two small lazy backs, or backrests, to convert the rockaway to an open-air vehicle. The cross-straps in the back are adorned with a brass medallion called a "back cross-strap center." The book steps, carpeted to match the interior, are attached to the doors with jointed irons and work automatically with the action of the door. The fine cut-glass lamps were made by A. P. DeVoursney of New York.

The interior is trimmed in green wool and broadlace. Fittings include green silk curtains, leather-covered door handles, a leather calling-card case and ivory slides for the window pulls. The roof is lined with diamond-patterned green wool, which extends to the roof over the driver's seat. The wool rug has a multicolored geometric pattern.

The vehicle is suspended on elliptic and French platform springs. The cut-under arch panel and absence of a reach allow the front wheels a full turning radius, called a "full lock," for maneuverability. The thin pump handles terminate in sharp points. Like the body, the gear is painted black with gold striping.

Documents that accompany this gift from the donor, a relative of the original owner, indicate that the vehicle was purchased by Mr. Marx Wintjin in 1871 and customized for his wife's personal use. The original bill of sale lists the price as $725 and stipulates that the vehicle was "warranted 1 year on the Road or 6 months on the Pavements." The rockaway was stored in the family's carriage house in New York City for four generations, until its donation to The Museums.

Detail of the coupé rockaway, with shifting front in place behind the driver's seat.

✿ GYPSY WAGON

23. Gypsy Wagon

Maker unknown, possibly New England;
1860–1885; 168 × 109 × 79 in
(427 × 297 × 201 cm); Exterior partially
restored, undercarriage and interior trim
restored 1955; Museums purchase, 1955

Gypsies, a distinct linguistic and cultural group, are thought to have originated in northern India. Among several subgroups, those who settled in Europe migrated via the Middle East and reached England during the sixteenth century. Most Gypsies in North America are descendants of British Gypsies who settled in the United States and Canada during the mid- to late nineteenth century. They made their living as horse traders, fortune-tellers and peddlers; contrary to the public stereotype of Gypsies as nomadic people, many in the United States had permanent residences. During the Carriage Era, when the demand for horses was high, some families established sales stables near urban areas.

Gypsy wagons, sometimes called wardos, were used for traveling, for fortune-telling and as residences. Although some of these vehicles were imported from England, many appear to have been made by American carriage manufacturers; however, only a few survive, because of the Gypsy custom of burning the possessions of an individual after death.[1]

The upper portion of the body of this wardo, well above the wheels, forms a ledge that extends beyond the track of the wheels in width to provide additional interior space. Access to the interior was gained by step plates attached to either side of the fore carriage and through the folding window panels at the front. The driver sat on the right interior bench seat where the brake lever is located; the reins passed through the open windows.

The narrower, lower part of the body is painted red. The chamfered, ribbed panels are accentuated by gold striping. The top and bottom of this section are framed with applied half-spindles with abstract leaf patterns in gold in each segment. The ledges are supported by four scrolled brackets on each side. The back has a curved luggage rack, or cradle, attached by hinges and leather straps.

The front and rear panels and the folding windows are decorated with small landscape and figurative paintings. The lower part of the ledge is red, decorated with half-spindles, beaded molding and painted four-leaf clovers in gold. The upper sides are covered in a heavy canvas painted light green. Large landscape paintings on each side, framed by painted scrollwork, are flanked by identical windows of frosted glass etched in a floral pattern. The windows, which can be lowered into the body, are mounted in a wooden sash framed by beaded molding. The upper sections of the front are fitted with red- and blue-tinted lancet windows. The rear window, tinted red and etched with an eagle with outspread wings, is also flanked by red and blue lancet windows. The tinted glass diffuses the interior with a rich, colored light.

The interior has a rear platform, used as a bed, with turned wooden railings and posts and a storage compartment underneath. The floor is painted in stripes. The top ledges of the bench seats are painted in orange and yellow squares outlined in black. Sprays of flowers are painted on the paneling above the seats. The restored interior trim consists of plush and crushed velvet applied to the walls and ceiling.

The body is hung on platform springs. The undercarriage is red, accented with gold striping. The spring blocks, crossbars, brake blocks and cradle ends terminate in carved eagle heads.

This vehicle belonged to Mrs. Phoebe Stanley, sometimes known as Gypsy Queen Phoebe, a resident of West Natick, Massachusetts. A newspaper story in the April 4, 1940, issue of the *Springfield Republican* notes that the late Mr. Thomas Stanley had been a horse trader and that Mrs. Stanley, interviewed in 1939 during the sale of the wardo, reported that she purchased the vehicle from a Taunton, Massachusetts, carriage maker for the sum of $2,500. In 1939 the wardo was reported to be in poor condition, having been stored in a light shed that had disintegrated during the 1938 hurricane. Mrs. Stanley died in 1939, just a few months after she sold the vehicle.[2]

[1]Matt Salo, Post-doctoral Fellow, Division of Community Life, National Museum of American History, Smithsonian Institution. Letter to Laura Gombieski, February 14, 1986. Information obtained from many newspaper accounts.
[2]*The Springfield Union*, April 4, 1940 (Springfield, Massachusetts).

Interior of the Gypsy wagon

COACHMAN-DRIVEN VEHICLES

Industrialization in the United States during the second half of the nineteenth century created new markets for luxury goods. While members of the middle class could purchase the now-affordable carriages for personal use that were mass produced in factories, wealthier individuals turned to luxury vehicles, many of which were designed to be driven by coachmen. American-made vehicles of this class were understated in appearance, with subtle, if not somber, exteriors. The expression of luxury was reserved for carriage interiors, which were trimmed in silk, satin and morocco and edged in the finest broadlace. Customers could order optional accessories such as folding vanities, cigar boxes and even vases for fresh-cut flowers.

During the height of the Carriage Era in the United States, approximately 1850 to 1910, coachman- and owner-driven vehicles filled carriage houses in cities and in fashionable summer resorts. These vehicles were as integral a part of social life as the fashions and the behavior advocated in the etiquette books or social guides of the day. The size and conformation of the horses, the proportion and finish of the carriage, the fit of the harness and the neatness of the coachman's and the groom's livery were prescribed as indicators of good taste. As described by James Garland in his book *The Private Stable*:

> *Good taste in a turn-out is shown by the choice of a properly designed carriage for the service it is intended to perform. The horse or the pair should be sound, well mannered, up to and not above the work; the harness simple, well made and properly put on; the servant or servants well appearing, well trained and uniformed in properly fashioned livery.*[1]

City parks were developed during this period, following English fashion and the public demand for healthful recreation. New York's Central Park, for example, built between 1857 and 1876, was designed for carriage driving as much as for the enjoyment of less affluent pedestrians. The owners of elegant vehicles delighted in driving in the park, an arena for displaying to onlookers their wealth, status and taste through the fittings of their vehicles and attendants. Walt Whitman penned a mixed reaction to this display of wealth after a visit to Central Park in May 1879:

> *Ten thousand vehicles careening through the Park this perfect afternoon. Such a show! and I have seen all—watch'd it narrowly and at my leisure. Private barouches, cabs and coupés, some fine horseflesh—lap dogs, footmen, fashions, foreigners, cockades on hats, crests on panels—the full oceanic tide of New York's wealth and 'gentility.'*[2]

The coachman who drove such elegant vehicles was essential to the management of both the vehicles and the horses that contributed to the social status of his employer and was expected to be proficient in a variety of duties. Ideally, his training started at an early age, perhaps 12 or 13, when his responsibilities included making fires, beating horse blankets, cleaning stalls, caring for harness and burnishing bits. Training in stable management preceded training in carriage driving. Owners were advised to oversee the stable help to prevent such not uncommon behavior as tormenting horses and indulging in alcohol. Garland warned, "coachmen and grooms do not form a class from which angels are exclusively chosen."[3]

The size, weight and appearance of the coachman and groom were dictated by fashion to fit the proportions of a particular carriage. The coachman's conduct had to be exemplary and his workday was often long. In addition to daily care of the

Brougham *1893; from* Illustrated Souvenir of the Studebaker Brothers Mfg. Co.; *Studebaker Bros., South Bend, Indiana; Museums Carriage Reference Library*

horses, when a carriage was called for at a specific time the coachman and other stable help prepared the horses, harness and vehicle, harnessed the horses and attired themselves in appropriate livery. The coachman was expected to wait for long periods of time while his employer paid social visits, shopped or attended dinner parties and balls.

Among the vehicles described are one French- and three American-made carriages built for the Vanderbilts; others were once owned by the Gardiner and Van Rensselaer families. Five of these vehicles were built by the New York firm of Brewster & Company, the preeminent carriage builder of luxury vehicles during the last half of the nineteenth century.[4] Not included from The Museums collection are such coachman-driven vehicles as the sociable, the landau and the barouche.

[1]James Garland, *The Private Stable* (Boston: Little, Brown and Co., 1903) 10.

[2]Elizabeth Barlow with Vernon Gray, Roger Pasquier and Lewis Sharp, *Central Park Book* (New York: The Central Park Task Force, 1977) 116.

[3]Garland, *The Private Stable*, 313.

[4]Carriages which bore the name "Brewster" were associated with superb materials, excellent design, and outstanding crraftsmanship. The founder of this tradition was James Brewster (1788–1866). In 1810, Brewster, after serving an apprenticeship in Massachusetts, established his own carriage-making firm in New Haven, Connecticut. In 1829, he opened a repository in New York City, with John R. Lawrence as partner. The New Haven factory burned in 1836, and in 1838, James Brewster formed a partnership with his son James B. Brewster, and started making carriages in New York City under the name James Brewster and Sons; Brewster's second son, Henry, joined the firm before 1850. The factory in New Haven was relocated to Bridgeport, operating under the name of James Brewster & Company. Henry left the firm in 1856, and entered into partnership with James Lawrence and John W. Britton; this firm was called Brewster & Company, and was located on Broome Street, New York City. In 1883, the sons of Henry Brewster and John W. Britton joined the firm, and in 1888, purchased the interests of Brewster & Company.

After 1856, James B. Brewster continued a rival company called J. B. Brewster and Company, which failed in 1895. Brewster & Company continued to prosper. In 1910, it relocated to Long Island City, where it manufactured both carriages and motorcars. Rolls Royce purchased Brewster & Company in 1925.

24. Coach

James Brewster and Sons, Broadway,
New York, New York; c. 1848
135 × 85 × 67 in (343 × 216 × 170 cm)
Exterior, interior original; Gift of The
Brooklyn Museum, Brooklyn, New York, 1961

The appearance of this coach represents carriage design in a transitional phase. Its silhouette resembles illustrations of early English coaches referred to as clarences or sovereigns, which remained popular until the 1870s. By the mid-nineteenth century the nomenclature for styles of enclosed vehicles such as coupés, broughams and clarences became ambiguous and contingent upon the choice of individual manufacturers. This elegant example represents a type of vehicle that reflected the social standing of well-to-do owners. Such vehicles featured understated exteriors and extremely lavish interiors, providing a high degree of luxury, comfort and privacy to the passengers.

The body is distinguished by a sharp C-curve, which breaks the line of the lower front panels. The upper quarter panels and undercarriage are painted black; the lower quarter panels and boot are reddish brown. The back has a footman's seat, red-tasseled

footman's pulls, a pageboard and an essentially decorative, functionally obsolete sword case. The oblong design of the door handle is repeated in the shape of the low mounting step and the padded mudguards. The coachman's seat is trimmed in leather. The footboard is finished with a patterned, painted carpet covered by an in-grain wool carpet in an abstract floral design.

The interior is trimmed in a tufted, off-white wool bordered with wide broadlace. The window lifters and the holders—the straps used by passengers to assist their entry into the carriage—are also trimmed in broadlace. The window slides and door handles are carved ivory. The windows have white silk curtains and the floor is covered with a pile carpet in a bold, colorful design.

The body is suspended on scroll end elliptic springs in front and scroll end French platform springs at the rear. The C-curve of the lower body panels and the absence of a perch allow the front wheels to pass under the body for a smaller turning radius. The James B. Brewster trademark, indicating that the manufacturer was located at that time at 396 Broadway in New York City, appears on the wheel hubs. The undercarriage is painted black with gold striping.

This coach was owned by the Gardiners, a prominent New York family descended from Lion Gardiner, an English officer entrusted with the fortification of Boston in 1635 who purchased Gardiner's Island, off the eastern shore of Long Island, in 1639. The coach remained in the family until it was donated to The Brooklyn Museum in 1943 by Miss Sarah Diodati Gardiner. Family tradition relates that the coach was purchased in 1833 to transport Miss Mary Brainerd Gardiner from East Hampton, New York, to Columbia, South Carolina. Design characteristics and the trademark indicate that the vehicle was probably made in the late 1840s.

25. Coach

James Goold & Company, Albany, New York
c. 1850; 158 × 84 × 70 in (401 × 218 × 178 cm)
Exterior restored prior to 1953; interior
original, with storm curtains restored 1955
Gift of the Franklin Institute, Philadelphia,
Pennsylvania, 1953

James Goold of Albany, New York, was one of the best-known American carriage manufacturers of the nineteenth century. He began his career in 1804 as an apprentice to William Clark and Jason Clapp, coach makers in Pittsfield, Massachusetts. In 1813 he set up a carriage-making shop in Albany, New York. For a century James Goold &

Company made a wide variety of carriages for the American market and became famous for the swelled-body sleighs that were known as albany cutters (see Cat. Nos. 55 and 59). James Goold was active in his business until his death in 1879 at the age of 90; his son and grandsons carried on the business until 1913.

The roof of this coach is somewhat flattened. Boots are located under the coachman's seat and at the rear, under the hind servants' seat. The body is painted green and black and the toeboard is flanked by ornamental metal handles. The door handles are silver-plated, as is the long step to the driver's seat. The step plate carries the maker's trademark.

The spacious interior is trimmed in brown leather lined with gold damask. The doors have glass windows. Exterior leather storm curtains lined in damask are hung at the front and rear quarter panel windows. Silk roll-up curtains are provided on the interior for additional privacy. The coach is mounted on telegraph and elliptic springs. It was made by Goold for his friend Stephen Van Rensselaer, III, a member of the prominent Albany, New York, family.

26. Town Coach

Maker unknown, United States; c. 1860
157 × 85 × 70 in (399 × 216 × 178 cm)
Exterior restored, interior incompletely
restored 1957; Museums purchase, 1955

This type of coach was designed for private use in the city. The upper quarter panels are painted black; the lower quarter panels are maroon. Both the body and the undercarriage are striped in red. The coachman's seat is mounted on curved and decorative iron stays placed over a Salisbury boot. The steps are mounted on hinged iron shanks that fold into a track under the floor of the body; the action of opening the door brings the shanks and step pads forward.

The body is set on long, sweeping iron arms resting on crossbars carved in an intricate rose and leaf decoration that is repeated in other iron and wooden members of the undercarriage. The vehicle is suspended on elliptic and French platform springs.

All interior trim was removed in preparation for restoration; the remnants of the original trim that are preserved in the collection indicate that the interior was trimmed in maroon satin.

27. Chariot D'Orsay
Million & Guiet, Paris, France; c. 1880
150 × 90 × 72 in (381 × 299 × 183 cm)
Exterior restored probably 1961; interior
original; Museums purchase, 1961

The term *chariot* was applied in ancient times to two-wheel vehicles used for war, for racing and for ceremony. About 1650 the name was resurrected and applied to elegant half-coaches characterized by an elevated body and high wheels. Lighter and less expensive than full coaches, chariots were popular luxury vehicles in the eighteenth and nineteenth centuries. This version was named after its designer, Alfred Guillaume Gabriel Count D'Orsay (1801–1852), a French dandy and arbiter of taste. It was designed to be used as a dress carriage for making formal calls.

The body is painted black and dark red, with striping in a lighter red. All exterior hardware is silver-plated. The silver drop handles on the doors are edged in a raised, graduated beading and carry the monogram of the owner.

The interior is trimmed in maroon silk satin edged in pasting lace. The window lifter, holders and borders are three-inch-wide striped grosgrain and satin broadlace ending in a deep twisted silk fringe. The sides and interior panels contain storage pockets. The upholstery buttons are covered wtih silk rosettes. The interior has ivory fittings and special wood cases for holding such items as calling cards. Stable shutters and silk shades can be drawn for privacy or to block the sun. The folding steps are covered in intricately tooled morocco leather and maroon satin.

The chariot is hung on a double suspension of C- and elliptic springs; a check strap is connected to the body to reduce swaying motion. This vehicle was owned by William K. Vanderbilt, a member of the New York Coaching Club and a noted whip, who resided in New York City and Oakdale, Long Island.

28. Circular Front Coupé

J. B. Brewster & Company, East 25th Street,
New York, New York; c. 1860
122 × 77 × 67 in (310 × 196 × 170 cm)
Exterior, interior original; Gift of Ward
Melville, 1971

Interior of the coupé,
showing the open vanity
drawer.

The term *coupé*, from the French meaning "cut," refers to the practice of cutting down or reducing the designs of larger coaches to produce a variety of smaller though still elegant enclosed vehicles. In the United States the terms *coupé* and *brougham* were frequently used interchangeably in the late nineteenth century.

This example is typical of the elegant coupés that were beautifully trimmed and appointed for private use. The body and undercarriage are painted black, and the latter is striped in red. The vehicle has beveled glass windows and exquisite silver-plated lamps with etched glass.

The interior shows the finest crafts-manship. The diamond-pleated burgundy satin interior is elaborately trimmed with maroon, pink and green patterned broad-lace, tassels and rosettes. The interior door handle and calling-card case are covered in a russet leather. The vehicle is furnished with deep sidewall pockets for storage, maroon satin window curtains and a mirrored vanity drawer that recedes into a compartment under the driver's seat boot. A small hinged child's seat is concealed behind the uphol-stered panel under the vanity. A bell pull is provided to signal the driver. Patterned wool carpet in green, maroon and yellow covers both the interior and the driver's seat floors.

The coupé is mounted on French platform springs at the rear and elliptic springs at the front. A manufacturer's label pasted under the interior seat indicates that the carriage's serial number is 2309, that the weight is 884 pounds and that the vehicle was made by the "Old House of Brewster/65 East 25th Street."

According to information received from the grandson of the original owner, this brougham was a gift to his grandmother, Mrs. Catherine Elizabeth Hartung, from her sons and was used in the funeral procession held for Abraham Lincoln in New York City in 1865.

29. Circular Front Brougham

Brewster & Company, Broome Street, New York, New York; c. 1880; 133 × 79 × 66 in (338 × 201 × 168 cm); Exterior, interior original; Gift of Ward Melville, 1971

The prototype of the brougham was designed by Lord Peter Henry Brougham of England in 1838 and made by the London coach builder Robinson. These four-wheel enclosed vehicles for two or more passengers remained popular throughout the Carriage Era in Europe and the United States. Broughams were also used as public cabs for hire.

This example is typical of the understated elegance preferred by the elite of the late nineteenth century. The body is painted dark green and black. Ornamentation is restrained and consists of dark blue striping and a small monogram, "JNN" or "INN," painted in green on the doors. The windows are framed in mahogany.

The interior is trimmed in black leather, with black and green broadlace. The carpet, curtains and driver's seat are also black. The brougham is equipped with a calling-card case on one door, an oval mirror mounted on a sidewall panel and a jump seat concealed by a leather panel below the rounded front window. A leather bell pull on this panel connects to the bell beneath the driver's seat, which was used to signal the coachman.

The brougham is suspended on elliptic and French platform springs. The manufacturer's serial number is 1957. The location of the manufacturer is stamped on the hubcaps.

30. Summer Brougham

Brewster & Company, New York, New York
1901; 128 × 80 × 61 in (325 × 203 × 155 cm)
Exterior, interior original; Gift of Ward
Melville, 1971

Summer broughams could be converted from enclosed vehicles to open vehicles by removing the upper quarter panels and lowering the windows into recesses in the door panels. They were popular for use in the country.

This example has painted, imitation caning on the rear lower quarter panels. Hand-painted caning was applied line by line and covered with several coats of glazes and varnish to produce a light and pleasing effect. The rest of the body is painted black and maroon with red striping, the stable colors of the Vanderbilts of New York. The monogram "AGV" is painted in red on the door.

The interior is trimmed in "camels hair"—a tan-colored canvas-like fabric—and the interior panels are covered in woven rattan caning. The vehicle is suspended on elliptic springs.

Brewster Company records indicate: "Serial number 243401/Country brougham/ Begun: February 27, 1901/Finished: September 18, 1901/Sold: September 24, 1901 to A. G. Vanderbilt/Drawing #22458 Sales Book No. 2, p. 102/Weight: 960 lbs./Price: $1,200."[1] It is one of several vehicles in The Museums collection that belonged to A. G. Vanderbilt (see Cat. Nos. 31, 32, 40, 47, and 52).

[1] Brewster & Company, Specification Book #13, Sales Book 2 (New York Public Library) 102.

Interior of the summer brougham

31. Station Brougham

Brewster & Company, New York, New York
1904; 128 × 81 × 66 in (325 × 206 × 168 cm)
Exterior, interior original; Gift of Ward
Melville, 1971

Standard broughams, for private use or for hire, were often adapted for transporting passengers to and from the railroad station by the addition of a luggage rack on the roof.

This privately-owned example has a slightly bowed roof reinforced with rows of wooden ribs. With the exception of the back panel, the vehicle is entirely enclosed by glass windows, which can be lowered into the panels below. The brougham can be converted to an open-air vehicle by removing the rear panel windows as well. It is painted maroon with red striping; the monogram "AGV" appears on both doors.

The interior is trimmed in a white wool fabric with white wool carpeting on the floor. Deep side pockets and a recessed compartment under the front window provide space for the smaller belongings of passengers. A pair of leather-covered clamps above this compartment held umbrellas or parasols. The vehicle is suspended on elliptic and French platform springs.

Although this brougham bears Alfred Gwynn Vanderbilt's monogram, Brewster Company records indicate serial number 22170 was sold originally to James Hazen Hyde on November 3, 1899,[1] also a member of the New York Coaching Club. It can be assumed that the brougham was returned to Brewster, credited to the purchase of another vehicle and refurbished to the specifications of Alfred G. Vanderbilt.

[1]Brewster & Company, Specification Book #10, Sales Book 26 (New York Public Library) 167.

32. Panel Boot Victoria

Brewster & Company, New York, New York
1903; 132 × 105 × 77 in (335 × 267 × 196 cm)
Exterior original; interior probably restored
prior to 1951; Gift of Ward Melville, 1971

These open, four-wheel vehicles with folding tops were of English origin and were also known as cabriolets. This version was named by the French to honor Queen Victoria of England (reigned 1837–1901) about 1844. It is characterized by a low-slung body for easy access and graceful lines. It was a preferred vehicle for park driving, since its open body and folding hood afforded a good view of the passengers. Many victorias had a skeleton boot supporting the coachman's seat that could be removed for more formal occasions when the victoria was driven postilion.

This example is painted black, maroon and red, and has the monogram "AGV." The low steps are attached to sweeping mud guards, which conform to the curved lines of the body. The interior has a painted carpet in red, maroon, black and gold, covered with a wool carpet in maroon. The trim is of plum-colored wool, bordered in satin broadlace. A carpeted folding child's seat is located at the rear of the panel boot, the storage compartment under the driver's seat.

The victoria is suspended on elliptic front springs and French platform springs at the rear; it has square carved pump handles. It was sold to Alfred Vanderbilt on November 13, 1903.[1] Brewster & Company's serial number for this vehicle is 25234.

[1]Brewster & Company, Specification Book #17, Sales Book 4 (New York Public Library) 383.

33. Summer Vis-a-Vis

Brewster & Company, New York, New York
1905; 132 × 82 × 60 in (335 × 208 × 152 cm)
Exterior, interior original; Museums
purchase, 1951

This popular and versatile summer vehicle was called a "sociable" in England and, by the nineteenth century, "vis-a-vis" in the United States, from the French phrase for "face to face." The vehicle came in a wide variety of designs, with or without doors, fixed, folding or parasol tops. The bodies were constructed of paneled wood or wicker.

This example has a natural, varnished wood finish and a fixed roof. The front and rear have glass windows and the side curtains, which are of beige waterproof canvas, can be drawn back with leather straps or fixed on brass knobs on the exterior. The vehicle has a wooden dash and mud guards. The doors carry a painted emblem, a human hand gripped in a bear's claw—the family crest of the original owner, H. Carroll Brown. H. Carroll Brown was a descendant of Charles Carroll of Maryland, a signer of the Declaration of Independence. The family's late-eighteenth-century estate, Brooklandwood, just north of Baltimore, had horse-racing stables and was the site of the Brookland Meet and the Maryland Hunt during the late nineteenth and early twentieth centuries.

The interior is trimmed in beige "camels hair" and has a beige wool floor carpet. The vehicle is suspended on elliptic springs. The ironwork is painted black; handles and other ornamental hardware are brass.

Brewster & Company records indicate: "Serial number 25000 New extra light Curtain Vis-a-Vis/Begun: September 6, 1904/ Finished: March 16, 1905/Sold: April 6, 1905 to H. Carroll Brown/Drawing #25000 Sales book No. 4, p. 184/Weight: 924 lbs./Price: $1,500."[1]

[1]Brewster & Company, Specification Book #17, Sales Book 4 (New York Public Library) 184.

PLEASURE DRIVING VEHICLES

Considerable ability and knowledge of horses were required to drive a carriage safely and effectively. Whether driving a vehicle harnessed to a single, pair, tandem or four, the driver, or "whip," had to be able to maneuver around obstacles, anticipate potential hazards that could cause a horse to shy, and respond to mishaps that could lead to serious accidents. The pleasure obtained from driving was directly proportional to improvements in roads and carriage design. As carriages and the surfaces they traversed were improved, better-bred and more spirited types of horses were used. Sport and recreational driving, which came to be known as "pleasure driving," began during the eighteenth century. The two most significant indications of this emerging activity were the development of the phaeton, one of the first carriages to be driven exclusively by their owners, and the growing interest in coaching at the end of the eighteenth century.

The term *phaeton*, first used in 1742, was applied to vehicles with precariously high suspension systems and with open bodies and forward-facing seats. The term was derived from the mythological Greek figure Phaeton, or Phaidon, the son of the sun-god Helios, whose reckless driving of his father's sun-chariot nearly set the world on fire. Eighteenth-century phaetons were indeed dangerous conveyances.

That it was dangerous clearly appears, and it was this very danger which must have contributed not a little to its popularity. It was driven at a very great rate, and with recklessness that excited the anger of the commoner folk—unless, as was often the case, it excited their admiration instead. The phaeton was the most sporting carriage you could have. It lent itself to the idea of racing, and there was always the chance that an accident might be fatal—an allurement in itself.[1]

The distinctive features of the eighteenth-century phaetons were their exaggerated height and the fact that they were owner-driven. It was not uncommon for these phaetons to be drawn at reckless speeds by four or more horses. In 1824 King George IV of England introduced a type that was considerably lower and pulled by ponies; vehicles patterned after this type were called George IV phaetons. By the mid-nineteenth century the distinctions of the phaeton were retained only through its name and nostalgic association, and the term was applied to over a dozen different styles of carriages, such as the mail phaeton, spider phaeton and basket phaeton.

Concurrent with the introduction of the phaeton was the emerging fashion of coaching. Young aristocrats learned to "handle the ribbons" from skilled coachmen on mail or stagecoaches. As reported by Nimrod, the famous sportsman of the Regency period:

From the art of driving four horses in hand—and an art it is, and by no means an easy one—I have not only derived an abundance of pleasure, but from the great practice I at one time had on public coaches, which their proprietors allowed me to drive, I so far perfected myself in the art as to enable me to commit the result of my experience to paper, never failing to assert the claims of coach-horses to the kindness of their drivers in the first place.[2]

Young noblemen also imitated the mannerisms and mode of dress of public coachmen. The mania for coaching led to the formation of numerous driving clubs in England, such as the Bensington Driving Club in 1807; the Richmond Driving

Club, founded in 1838 by Lord Chesterfield (who advised members to *drive* like coachmen but *look* like gentlemen); and the Four-in-Hand Club in 1856.

The New York Coaching Club was founded in 1875 and held its first public parade meet in Madison Square on April 22, 1876. The event was recorded by Coaching Club member Reginald Rives:

The whole neighborhood around Madison Square seemed suddenly to become possessed of unusual charms, for sportsmen of all classes and men, whose faces are familiar to the "frequenters" of the Road and the loungers at the "Monico" (Delmonico's, Fifth Avenue and 26th Street) came dashing up in their T-carts, Dog-carts, Wagons and Phaetons, drawn by single horses, double teams, and tandems.[3]

Formal park drags and private road coaches were used in regular meets and annual parades and were exhibited at the National Horse Show at Madison Square Garden. The displays of immaculate turnouts, the excitement of the sound of horses' hooves and the rumble of rolling coaches made it a dramatic spectacle for the public.

Magnificent as to varnish, perfect as to appointments, and drawn by sprightly steeds, groomed to a point of shininess almost painful, the drags of the Coaching Club made a beautiful and imposing appearance, and their deck loads of beautiful ladies robed in the magnificence of spring attire, and the gentlemen glorifying in buttonhole bouquets and the charm of the Club uniform, added materially to the beauty of the scene.[4]

Ladies not only displayed their beauty and fashionable attire from the roof seats of coaches, but also demonstrated their driving skills. In 1901, the Ladies' Four-in-Hand Driving Club was formed and, like the Coaching Club, held regular meets, which often concluded with a luncheon at the Colony Club in New York.

The replacement of public mail coaches by the railroad as a basic form of transportation inspired a nostalgia for the precise timing between stops on a route that marked a skilled coachman. The Coaching Club in America re-created staging routes and celebrated members of the Club such as Colonel Delancey Astor Kane and Alfred Gwynn Vanderbilt drove public coaches.[5] In 1880 The New York Coaching Club commissioned Brewster & Co. of New York to build the road coach "Pioneer" as a conveyance for excursions for paying passengers.

Pleasure driving could entail a leisurely outing in an urban park or in the country with a single pony and a smart-looking road cart as well as a competitively timed coaching excursion. Vehicles used for pleasure driving included general transport vehicles such as the stanhope gig, tilbury or finer road wagons.

The catalog presents 20 examples of pleasure driving vehicles made between 1860 and 1925, and includes a variety of American- and European-made vehicles arranged by type. Included are phaetons, breaks, wagons, and private road coaches. Also included is a variety of two-wheel pleasure vehicles such as curricles, cabriolets, gigs and road carts. Not included from The Museums collections are a park drag, park phaeton and other specific styles of carts such as the whitechapel cart.

[1]Ralph Straus, *Carriages and Coaches* (London: Martin Secker, 1913) 195.
[2]Charles James Nimrod, *My Life and Times*, ed. with additions by E. D. Cuming (New York: Charles Scribner's Sons, 1927) 118.
[3]Reginald Rives, *The Coaching Club* (New York: privately printed, 1935) 2–3.
[4]Rives, 9.
[5]The objective of coaching, unlike that of racing, was to arrive at a specific destination exactly on time; to finish in less than the allowed time could cause injury to the horses.

34. George IV Phaeton

Brewster & Company, New York, New York
c. 1860; 113 × 60 × 58 in
(287 × 152 × 147 cm); Exterior partially
restored, interior restored 1951; Gift of Mrs.
Henry Lewis, III, Charles G. Meyer, Jr.,
G. Howland Meyer and S. Willits Meyer, in
memory of G. Howland Leavitt and his
daughter, Sara Willits Meyer, 1951

In 1824, King George IV of England, an avid sportsman in his youth, was in declining health. He requested his coach makers to design a vehicle that would be more easily accessible than the high phaetons that were popular among the aristocracy during the first half of the nineteenth century. The result was a low-hung vehicle with a gracefully curved body, small front wheels with a full lock and a groom's rumble seat in the back. In time, this variant of the phaeton became the preferred type for ladies to drive.

This phaeton is black and maroon, with vermillion striping and canework on the seat panels. It has a wide dash with a curved rein guide and a wedge seat with a locked compartment.

The vehicle is hung on four elliptic springs. The monogram "CMG," representing the name of a relative of the donors, appears on a raised boss on one side. A paper certificate pasted under the seat reads, "certificate of manufacture / First Prize of the London / Exhibition / 1862 / Awarded to Brewster & Co. / 11416."

35. Mail Phaeton

Peters & Sons, London, England; 1867
114 × 100 × 73 in (290 × 254 × 185 cm)
Exterior, interior original; hood and seat
restored 1982; Gift of the Estate of
Walter Jennings, 1951

The mail phaeton, so called because it utilized the springs developed for mail coaches, was popular in England in the 1830s as a sporting vehicle and for traveling. It is characterized by a square body, a folding top over the driver's seat and a rear seat large enough for two grooms.

This mail phaeton has a black body with seat panels covered with caning. It is mounted on heavy telegraph springs joined by leather robins. The gear is painted maroon.

The vehicle was built in 1867 for Baron Lionel de Rothschild of England (1808–1879), a banker and philanthropist. Its second owner was the noted American whip Burton Mansfield, known as the "father of the tandem," who acquired the phaeton in 1879. The monogram on the sides is that of the last owner, Walter Jennings (1858–1933), who was a director of the Standard Oil Company.

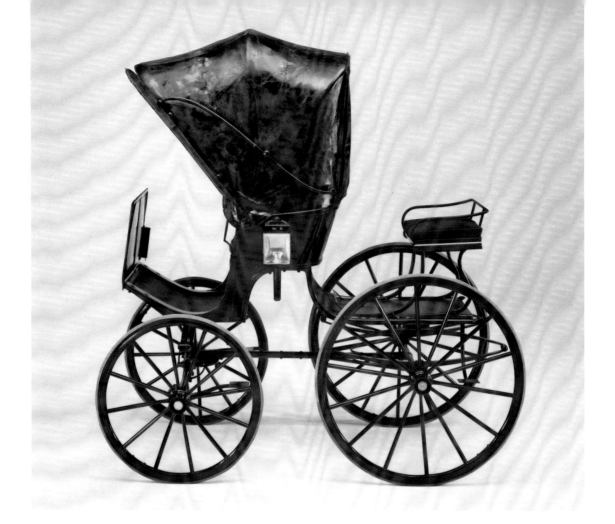

36. Spider Phaeton

Brewster & Company, New York; 1897
90 × 90 × 60 in (229 × 229 × 152 cm)
Exterior restored 1952; interior probably
restored prior to 1952; Gift of Elizabeth
Lamont, 1952

The spider phaeton was popular among gentlemen for pleasure driving and for competitive show driving. It is characterized by a tilbury body on four wheels, a folding top and a skeleton rumble seat for the grooms.

The body, which is cut-under for a full lock, is painted black with red striping. The interior trim is a green broadcloth. The phaeton is suspended on three elliptic springs and the undercarriage is also black.

Brewster & Company records indicate that this vehicle was built for Col. Daniel S. Lamont, who was a journalist and later the private secretary to President Grover Cleveland. Construction was begun on May 3, 1897, and it was sold on May 7, 1898.[1]

[1] Brewster & Company, Specification Book #9, Sales Book 25 (New York Public Library) 113.

37. Buckboard Phaeton

*Joubert & White, Glens Falls, New York
c. 1900; 115×90×65 in
(292×229×165 cm); Exterior, interior
restored, probably 1953; Gift of Charles
Alden Poindexter, 1953*

The buckboard, an American invention
of the early nineteenth century, was a four-
wheel vehicle with a simple body mounted
on long planks attached to the axles. The
seats attached directly to the floorboards.
The firm of Joubert & White introduced a
novel suspension system, which they
patented in 1880. The patent application
reads:

*Our invention relates to buckboard wagons; and
it consists of a self-supporting side-spring attachment as a 'riser': to raise the wagon body from
the boards or slats. . . . We avoid the otherwise
disagreeable tremble, rattling, and drumming of
the feet, cancelling or avoiding the most serious
objection to buckboard-wagons.[1]*

This pleasure vehicle combines a
phaeton body with a groom's rumble seat
and a buckboard undercarriage. The body is
made of varnished bird's-eye maple and it is
fitted with a leather folding top with leather
wings, or fenders. The step plates, axle clips
and other hardware are aluminum-painted.
The rumble seat is supported by a pair of
whip springs. The serial number 663 appears
on the seat.

[1]United States Patent Office, Patent No. 223,920,
January 27, 1880. Application filed December 18, 1879.

38. Basket Phaeton

A. T. Demarest & Company, New York, New York; c. 1895; 115×88×65 in (292×224×165 cm); Exterior, interior original; Museums purchase, 1959

The basket phaeton, of English origin, was a fashionable resort, park or beach carriage in America, driven almost exclusively by women in the late nineteenth century. The wicker work body, scrolled ironwork and curving lines gave it a light and graceful appearance. The sloping fenders and low entrance made the vehicle easily accessible to ladies in full skirts. Gentlemen's phaetons, in contrast, were of heavier construction and more angular design and were painted in darker colors.

This phaeton has a wicker body, fenders and dash and a rumble seat for the groom. The beige and burgundy parasol is decorated with a silk fringe. The phaeton is suspended on four elliptic springs and the maker's name appears on the hubs. It originally belonged to Miss Blanche Nolan of Saratoga and New York, New York.

Miss Nolan in her carriage, The Lawn, Saratoga, September 9, 1895; Museums collection

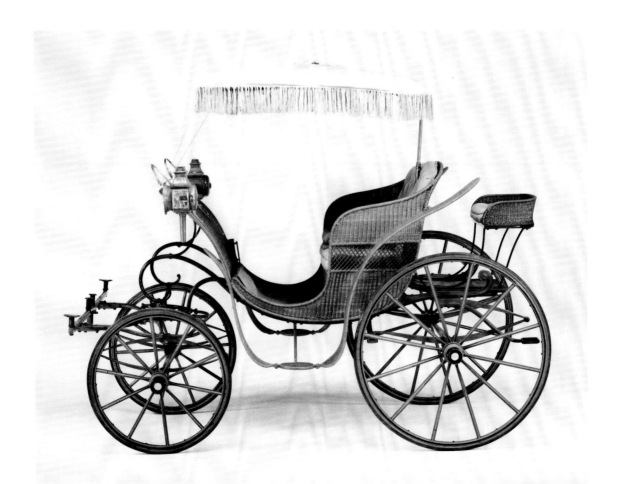

39. Basket Phaeton

Maker unknown, United States; c. 1900
74 × 75 × 55 in (188 × 191 × 140 cm)
Exterior restored 1954; interior original
Bequest of Marion T. Shotter, 1966

Developed in England, these small basket phaetons pulled by a single pony were popular in the United States for park driving and country use. The style of the body of this phaeton was referred to as a "Queen's Body Phaeton," patterned after a type made for Queen Victoria.

The body, dash and mud guards are of wicker. The beige parasol top, edged in silk fringe, can be removed or folded from a center joint on the support. The seat is trimmed in beige Bedford cord. The body is suspended on an iron frame and three elliptic springs. The undercarriage is painted red.

40. Dos-A-Dos Phaeton

*Brewster & Company, New York, New York
c. 1900; 86 × 63 × 58 in
(218 × 160 × 147 cm); Exterior, interior
original; trim probably restored; Gift of Mrs.
Byford Ryan, 1956*

Dogcart phaetons were four-wheel versions of the popular two-wheel dogcarts used in hunting (see Cat. No. 50). This dos-a-dos phaeton, a type of dogcart phaeton named for its back-to-back seating arrangement, was a small sporting vehicle designed to be used with a pair of ponies.

The body and undercarriage are painted black with double red striping on the undercarriage. The tailgate can be lowered to serve as a footboard for the passengers. It is fitted with a foot brake and rubber tires. The trim is burgundy wool.

The suspension consists of four elliptic springs. The cut-under body and the absence of a reach permit a full lock in turning. The Brewster & Company serial number is 25830. Brewster & Company records indicate that this vehicle was called a "dos-a-dos phaeton" and a "4 Wheel Game Cart." This vehicle weighed 473 pounds and was ordered by Alfred Gwynn Vanderbilt on June 30, 1908; construction was completed on September 30, 1908.[1]

[1]Brewster & Company, Specification Book #18, Sales Book 5 (New York Public Library) 355.

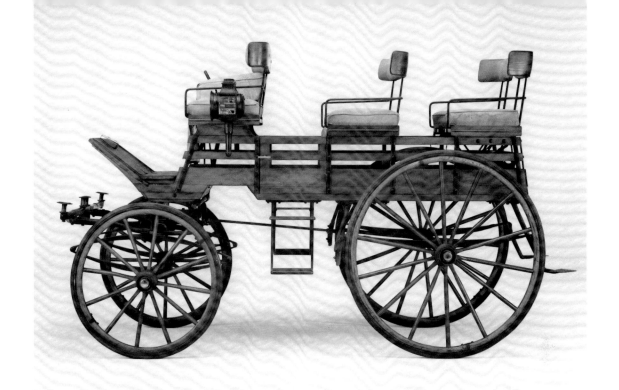

41. Slat-Side Mountain Phaeton

Brewster & Company, New York, New York
1904; 128 × 64 × 75 in (325 × 163 × 191 cm)
Exterior, interior original; Gift of
Mrs. William Walsh, 1984

This phaeton has slat sides and high seats. The body has a varnished wood finish and a boot beneath the driver's seat. The toeboard has a brass case for a clock. The doors, located between the first and second seats, are fitted with nickel-plated handles. The two rear seats are accessible from the hinged tailgate and rear side steps.

The trim is "camels hair;" the toeboard and tailboard are covered with linoleum. The body is suspended on elliptic and half-elliptic springs and the wheels are fitted with rubber tires. The undercarriage is also varnished wood.

Ware describes this vehicle as a "slat side mountain phaeton" under the category "Nondescript Carriages."[1] The vehicle's serial number is 24788; it is listed in the manufacturer's records as a "New Light Rand Break."[2] It was first sold to W. F. Cochran, and was subsequently owned by Joseph Wilshire, a noted American whip. (See Cat. Nos. 42 and 44).

[1]Francis T. Underhill, *Driving for Pleasure; or the Harness Stable and its Appointments* (New York: D. Appleton and Company, 1897) 158.
[2]Brewster & Company, Designs for Carriages 1893–1901 (The Metropolitan Museum of Art, New York, New York, accession no. 23.112.3; gift of William Brewster, 1923).

42. Wagonette Break

Brewster & Company, New York, New York
1898; 141 × 98 × 74 in (358 × 249 × 188 cm)
Exterior, interior original; Gift of
Mrs. William Walsh, 1984

The wagonette was popularized by Prince Albert of England, who used it as an outing vehicle for the royal family in the middle decades of the nineteenth century. The characteristic features of this popular, late-nineteenth-century pleasure carriage include longitudinally placed seats and a door at the rear.

This example, also known as a "body break," has a black body, with the toeboard and seat risers glazed in carmine and striped in black. The seats are trimmed in "tapes-try," an off-white wool with a scattered black pattern. The box seat is quite high, allowing the driver a good view of the horses. A hand brake is located next to the driver's seat. Storage compartments include a side pocket at the driver's seat and a spacious boot with a hinged door beneath the seat. A brass clock case is mounted on the toeboard. Both transverse seats have hinged lazy backs; the rear seat can be removed for lower seating on the longitudinal seats, which are backed by a seat rail with turned spindles. Access to the back is through the door at the rear, by way of a ladder mounted on one side near the axle.

The vehicle is suspended on telegraph springs. The rear axle has an odometer. The undercarriage is painted red with black striping. The manufacturer's serial number is 21547. Originally sold to Tracy Davis in 1898,[1] this vehicle subsequently belonged to the noted American whip Joseph Wilshire.

[1] Brewster & Company, Specification Book #9, Sales Book 25 (New York Public Library) 167.

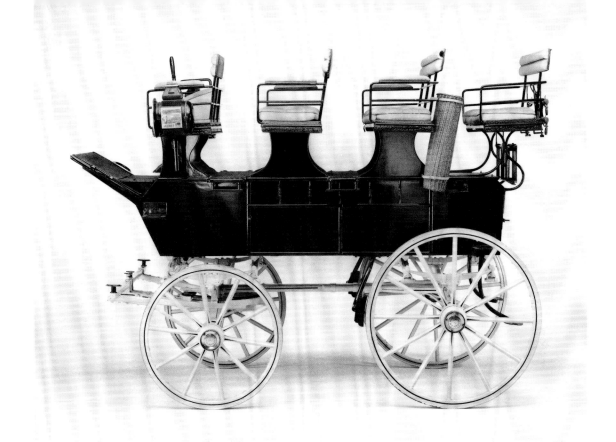

43. Roof-Seat Break

A. T. Demarest & Company, New York, New York; c. 1894; 132 × 105 × 77 in (335 × 267 × 196 cm); Exterior, interior restored 1952–1955; Gift of Ward Melville, 1971

The roof-seat break was adapted from the heavier vehicles that were used to break and train horses to harness (see Cat. No. 45). With the addition of seats on top of the box-like body and storage compartments, breaks like this one also functioned as pleasure vehicles for outings or as sporting vehicles to demonstrate the skill of the whip. The height of the seats made these vehicles popular at races and other spectator events, where they served as mobile grandstand seating.

The body, painted black, has a pair of large lamps made by the DeVoursey Company of New York. The commodious storage compartments at the rear contain two large mahogany chests with zinc-lined bottle racks; they once also held boxes with racks for dishes and glassware. Documents accompanying the vehicle indicate that the storage compartments could hold 100 pounds of ice and 47 bottles of wine.

The trim is beige Bedford cloth. The break is suspended on telegraph springs and the undercarriage is painted yellow with black striping. This break was ordered from the manufacturer by James Hoyt of Bellport, Long Island, in 1894. It was used for coaching trips to nearby towns and to the eastern end of Long Island, and frequently traveled on the Orient Point ferry across Long Island Sound to New London, Connecticut, for excursions to New England. It was acquired by Ward Melville from the owner's daughter.

44. Private Road Coach

Peters & Sons, London, England; c. 1925
150 × 98 × 86 in (381 × 249 × 218 cm)
Exterior, interior original; Gift of
Mrs. William Walsh, 1984

This privately-used road coach, known as the "Olden Time," is a splendid example of the type of vehicle that was used for the sport of four-in-hand driving by Colonel DeLancey Kane, Frederick Bronson, William Jay and other whips who founded

the New York Coaching Club. Club members held annual parades down Fifth Avenue in New York City and ran a series of public coaches for pleasure between various cities and resort areas. These coaches were reproductions of early English mail coaches. Club members also used these vehicles for private coaching trips for family and friends.

The upper body and boot panels are painted black; the lower panels are maroon. The toeboard, front seat panels and under-carriage are painted yellow with black striping. The coach has a hand brake and a drag shoe to slow the vehicle on steep downgrades. It is equipped with a wicker basket for umbrellas, walking sticks and a coaching horn; a folding step ladder; extra lead bars and large, brass-plated lamps made by Peters & Sons. The brass clock case on the toeboard held a clock or watch to assist the driver in maintaining a timed schedule. The doors are fitted with glass windows and stable shutters that can be lowered into slotted chambers in the door panels. The rear boot contains two large chests for wine racks and glassware; leather luggage straps are attached to the roof and the iron railings above the sides.

Back of the private road coach, showing mahogany wine glass racks

The exterior and interior seats are trimmed in "tapestry." The interior is paneled entirely in mahogany and features leather door pockets, a leather rack on the ceiling and rows of brass hooks for hats and other articles. The interior fittings are of ivory.

The initials "OT" above painted lead bars on the doors stand for "Olden Time," the name given to this road coach by its original owners, Mr. and Mrs. Joseph Wilshire of Connecticut. The late date of manufacture suggests that it was one of the last road coaches made in London at the end of the Carriage Era.

45. Skeleton Break

Brewster & Company, New York, New York 1901; 149 × 92 × 76 in (378 × 234 × 193 cm) Restored 1952–1955; Gift of Ward Melville, 1971

Although a break is not used for pleasure driving, it is a vehicle designed for training horses for carriage driving, and was an important vehicle in large private stables.

Great skill and care are required to train a horse to accept the weight of a vehicle, its motion, the accompanying noise and the commands of the driver; in addition, in order to work with other horses, whether hitched in a pair or in other combinations, a horse must learn how to assume his position in harness and to maintain balanced exertion and a steady pace.

The high seat of the skeleton break provides the driver with a full view of the horses for better control. A platform behind the seat carries assistants, who can dismount at a moment's notice and attend to unruly horses or to harness adjustments.

This break has a long, heavy perch and a wide track, features that contribute to the stability of the vehicle. It has a pair of elliptic springs at the front and no springs at the rear. The splinter bar is padded. A hand brake is provided to prevent the vehicle from overrunning the horses on steep downgrades. The break is painted maroon with wide vermillion striping; the hardware is painted black.

The carriage maker's serial number for this vehicle is 23308. Brewster & Company records indicate that this break was ordered by J. H. Moore in 1901, but was sold to H. B. Anderson on May 13, 1903.[1]

[1]Brewster & Company, Specification Book #13, Sales Book 3 (New York Public Library) 487.

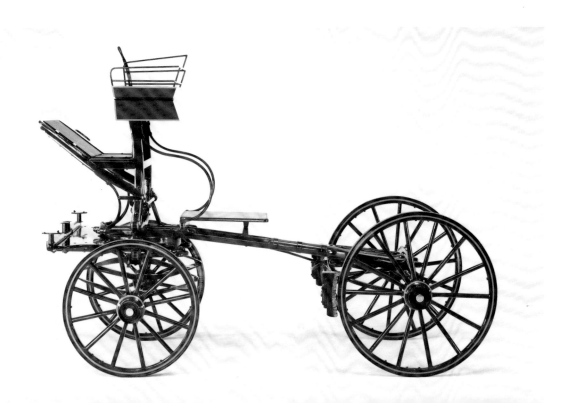

46. Laska Commissary Wagon

Henry Hooker & Company, New Haven, Connecticut; c. 1904; 98 × 68 × 76 in (249 × 157 × 193 cm); Exterior, interior restored, probably 1953; Gift of Edward L. Tinker, 1952

This type of gentleman's sporting vehicle was designed for hunting expeditions and was variously known as a hunting wagon, game wagon, four-wheel dogcart and commissary wagon—the latter designation borrowed from the commissary wagons used by the military to carry supplies and applied to a pleasure vehicle with interior storage for hunting gear and game.

This wagon has a cut-under body finished in varnished wood; the ironwork is painted cream color. It is fitted with a hand brake operated from the driver's seat. A brass-encased clock was once mounted on the footboard and the rear seat is both reversible and removable.

The vehicle is mounted on a pair of elliptic springs set parallel to the axles, which are connected by a reach. The hubcaps bear the trademark of Van Tassel & Kearney, the sole agents for Henry Hooker & Company in New York City during the 1890s.

The carriage manufacturer's 1904 catalog in The Museums Carriage Reference Library shows a shop drawing of this vehicle, which is described in the catalog as a "Laska Commissary Wagon," designed "especially for gentlemen's estates" and for exercising horses. Serial numbers 18659 and 1849 appear on this vehicle.

The monogram on the driver's seat panel has the initials "ELT," those of the donor. Prior to restoration, the monogram read "HCT," the initials of Henry C. Tinker, the donor's father and the previous owner of the wagon.

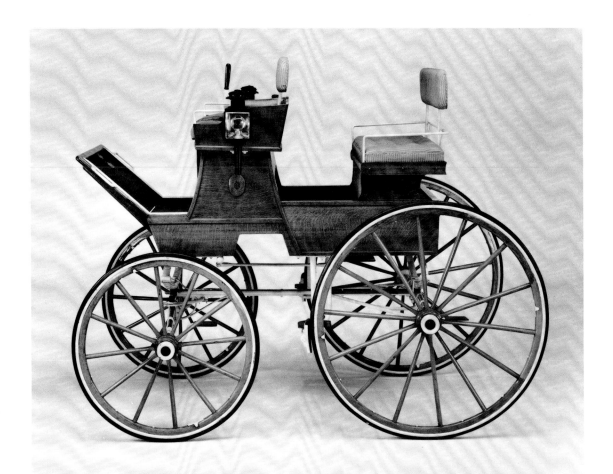

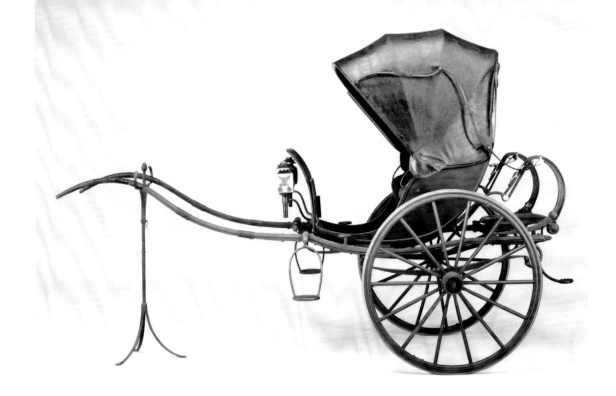

47. Cabriolet

Brewster & Company, New York, New York
1908; 151 × 93 × 65 in (384 × 236 × 165 cm)
Exterior, interior original; Gift of Ward
Melville, 1971

The term *cabriolet* is derived from the Latin *caprioles*, for "goat;" it was first applied to two-wheel Italian gigs in the seventeenth century. By the nineteenth century the name was used for a fashionable gentleman's vehicle.

A cabriolet required a horse that possessed considerable size, strength and high action. A diminutive groom, called a "tiger," stood on the footman's cushion at the rear. According to the dictates of fashion, the "tiger" could be no taller than the top bows of the extended folding hood.

The nautilus-shaped body of this cabriolet is painted maroon and black with vermillion striping. The hood is of long-grain leather and the hardware is silver-plated. The owner's monogram, "AGV," appears on the side panels.

The floor is carpeted with a low-pile maroon wool carpet over a patterned painted carpet. The long shafts extend to support graceful C-springs. The tires, of India rubber, carry the still-legible name of Brewster & Company.

This cabriolet was purchased in 1908 by Alfred G. Vanderbilt for the sum of $1,250. Its serial number is 25809. Brewster & Company records indicate that this vehicle was also called a "Cee Spring Hooded Gig" for "the youngsters." The original complete weight of the vehicle was 711 pounds.[1]

[1]Brewster & Company, Sepcification Book #18, Sales Book 5 (New York Public Library) 329.

48. Curricle

J. B. Brewster & Company, New York, New York; c. 1870; 105 × 100 × 74 in (267 × 254 × 188 cm); Exterior, interior original; Gift of Ward Melville, 1971

The term *curricle* is derived from the Latin *curriculum*, the name of a Roman racing chariot. In mid-eighteenth-century England it was applied to an elaborate gig or chaise pulled by a pair of horses. Curricles were used by fashionable gentlemen during the eighteenth and early nineteenth centu-ries, and a limited number of them continued to be produced through the early twentieth century for pleasure driving.

This curricle has a curved half-panel body articulated with vertical molding. It is painted dark green with blue striping. The long-grain leather folding top has silver-plated spiral prop nuts. A rumble seat is provided for grooms, with the step to the rumble offset to the left. The vehicle has two lamps with convex glass sides. The interior trim is a light beige broadcloth; the floor has a patterned, painted carpet with wool carpeting on the edges.

The curricle is mounted on C-springs and side springs. The crossbars have elongated scroll terminations. The hubcaps are incised with "Design Pat'd/J. B./Brewster/& Co./of 25th St. N.Y." The manufacturer's serial number for this vehicle is 7531.

49. Curricle

Million & Guiet, Paris, France; c. 1890
60 × 63 × 65 in (152 × 160 × 165 cm)
Restored, probably 1965; Gift of Francis R.
Appleton, Jr., 1964

The varnished mahogany panels of the square body of this vehicle are set off by painted black molding. The hinged toeboard and seat can be adjusted to the size of the driver and to balance the vehicle. The hinged tailgate provides access for passengers in the rear, where the seating is back-to-back.

The trim is blue broadcloth and the lazy back on the seat is of russet leather. The vehicle is suspended on side springs. The undercarriage is painted black with red striping. The hubcaps read "Million & Guiet/PARIS; 6099." The monogram on the sides is an "A" enclosed in a circle, the initial of the donor.

Francis R. Appleton Jr.
at Appleton Farms,
Ipswich, Massachusetts,
October, 1900; Museums
collection

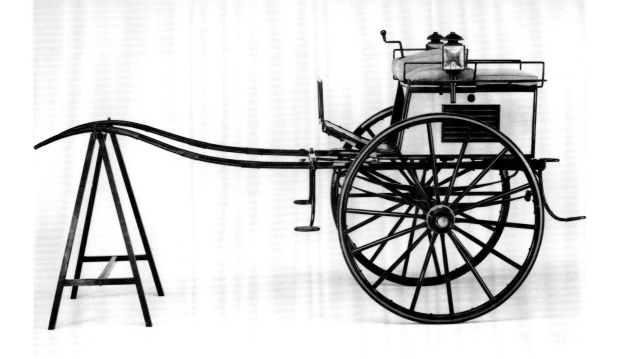

50. Dogcart
Brewster & Company, New York, New York
1902; 128 × 72 × 70 in (325 × 183 × 178 cm)
Exterior, interior restored 1953; Gift of
Elizabeth Lamont, 1952

Dogcarts were first used in England for transporting dogs and game for hunting. In the late nineteenth century the term was applied to a variety of two-wheel vehicles, partly because the designation permitted the owners to avoid the tax that was applied to pleasure vehicles. Many had the name of the owner and his occupation painted on the side as proof of their functional use. This vehicle was also called a "going to covert cart," from the title of a print by Charles Cooper Henderson which featured a cart of this design.

These vehicles were driven in tandem to fox hunts. The term *tandem* is Latin for "at length." The horse closest to the vehicle, the "wheeler," performs most of the work, while the "leader" horse, which is not in draft, is warmed up or "hacked" at a trot in front and then unhitched for riding at the hunt. Tandem driving had a limited popularity in England and the United States; it is considered the most hazardous form of driving because the leader is not restrained by the shafts and is thus more difficult to control.

This cart has carved imitation caning on the sides. A louvred panel on each side provides ventilation for the boot, where the dogs are carried. The tailboard can be lowered to serve as a toeboard for the rear passengers. A hand crank was employed to position the seats to balance the load imposed on the horse by additional passengers.

This dogcart was originally sold to Daniel S. Lamont in 1902. The manufacturer's serial number is 24112. Brewster & Company records indicate that the cart weighed 605 pounds. The vehicle is listed as a "Casset Cart."[1]

[1]Brewster & Company Specification Book #15, Sales Book 2 (New York Public Library) 463.

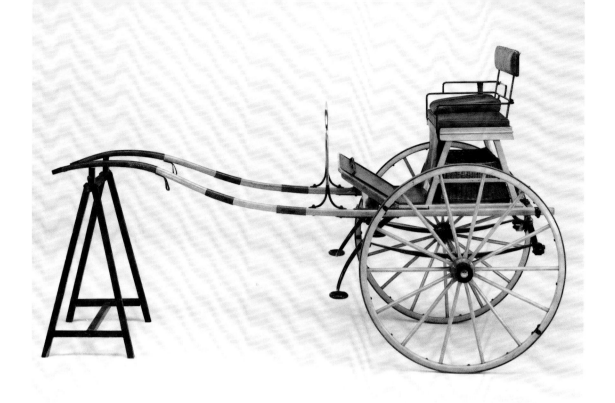

51. Gig

James Cunningham Son & Company,
Rochester, New York; c. 1895; 135 × 75 × 67
in (330 × 191 × 170 cm); Exterior, interior
restored 1955; Gift of James Cunningham
Son & Company, 1955

Gigs were a popular vehicle for traveling and for pleasure driving. They could be driven either in tandem or with a single horse.

This tandem gig has a varnished wood finish. The high seat is supported by A-frame pillars; the seat panels are decorated with beading. The open boot under the seat has a basketwork compartment. The vehicle lacks a dash, which would obstruct the driver's view of the horses; in its place is an open brass rein rail. The trace hooks attach to a spring behind the transom, a mechanism that absorbs some of the motion of the horse that would normally be transferred through the traces.

The gig is suspended on two side springs and a cross spring. The manufacturer's serial number is 1924.

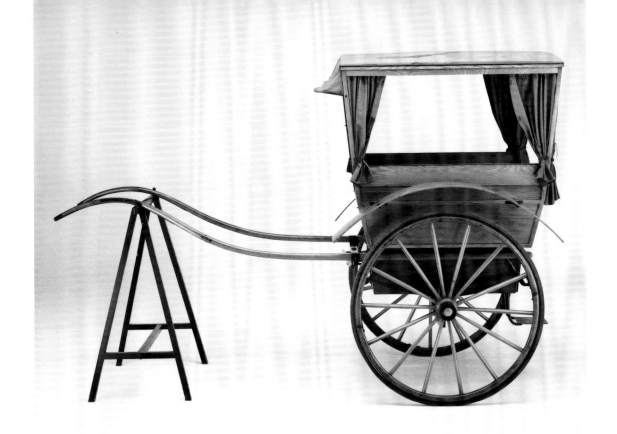

52. Inside Car

Brewster & Company, New York, New York
1902; 136 × 88 × 65 in (345 × 224 × 165 cm)
Exterior, interior original; Gift of Ward
Melville, 1971

The style of this vehicle was developed in Ireland. This cart has a body made of wide straight-grained wood panels finished in varnish. The body and lower door panels are mahogany; seat panels and upper door panels are hazel. The other sections are ash and hickory. The fixed top is supported by standing pillars. A shallow awning is attached to the front of the roof. The head lining is finished in caning, secured by one-inch half-round wooden battens. The interior trim is "camels hair." Rubberized canvas curtains, attached to the sides and the rear, can be closed during inclement weather.

The vehicle is suspended on side springs. Brewster & Company records describe this vehicle as an "inside car;" the vehicle weighed 481 pounds.[1] Its serial number is 23694. It was sold to Alfred G. Vanderbilt, member of the New York Coaching Club and a noted whip.

[1]Brewster & Company, Designs for Carriages 1893–1902 (The Metropolitan Museum of Art, accession no. 23.112.3; gift of William Brewster, 1923) pages for 1902.

53. East Williston Cart

*East Williston Cart Company, East Williston,
New York; c. 1895; 124 × 61 × 65 in
(315 × 155 × 165 cm) Exterior, interior
restored, probably 1964; Museums collection*

A number of two-wheel carts were
developed on Long Island during the late
nineteenth century. The mineola cart was
patented in 1885 by Charles Ellison; the east
williston cart was patented by Henry M.
Willis in 1891; Lyman W. Valentine, the
proprietor of the East Williston Cart
Company in 1895, later patented a vehicle
called the hempstead cart, although this
type was originally produced by Robert H.
Nostrand.

Henry M. Willis, born in Hempstead
in 1848, operated a livery establishment at
Orchard Hurst and, later, a business that
sold agricultural implements and windmills.
In his patent application for the east williston cart—No. 447,391, filed on June 16,
1890—he described his invention: "The
improvement is intended for that class of
two-wheeled vehicles known as 'carts' used
for racing, pleasure riding, and business
purposes, equipped with liberally-yielding
springs, and adapted for fast driving over
either smooth or rough roads."

The patent was granted for a vehicle
that incorporated an elastic U-shaped spring
attached to the shafts as well as a pair of
elliptic springs under the shafts. This U-
shaped spring absorbs the horse motion that,
in other vehicles, is usually transferred
directly from the horse to the vehicle
through rigid, fixed shafts. East williston
carts were very popular and were sold widely
throughout the United States, in Europe and
in South America. An advertisement in the
Queens County *Sentinel* on August 18, 1892,
called it "A Cart for the People" possessing
"Strength/Finish/Comfort/Durability," and
guaranteed "Absolutely no Horse-Motion."

The body has a varnished, natural
wood finish, typical brass hardware and a
brass mesh dash. The hinged seat folds
forward for access to the rear platform. The
seat backs are also hinged. The serial
number is 2153.

The east williston cart was ideally
suited for pleasure driving by both ladies and
gentlemen. It continues to be a popular
vehicle among carriage enthusiasts for both
pleasure and competitive driving.

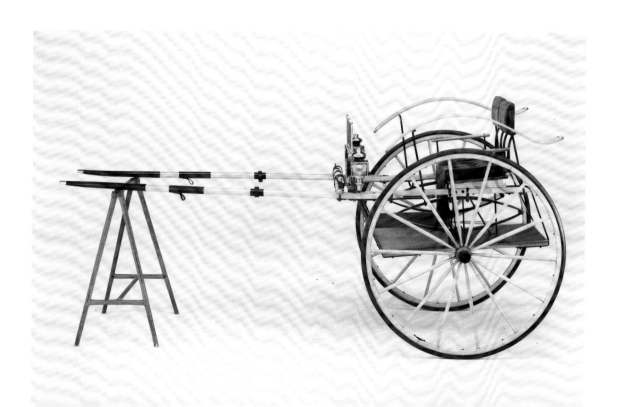

SLEIGHS

In the northern United States, the winter months were ideal both for travel and for pleasure driving, because packed snow and ice leveled the usually rough and difficult roads that contributed to the discomforts of early carriage travel. Quite in contrast to today's automobile drivers, Americans during the Carriage Era welcomed the first snowfall with enthusiasm.

The earliest American sleighs were open, box-like vehicles on runners and many of these "country sleighs" could be converted to freight vehicles by the removal of seat planks. There was more widespread ownership of sleighs than of wheeled carriages, probably because many sleighs were inexpensive and simply made and could be fashioned by local craftsmen. A variety of sleigh designs was developed during the nineteenth century for both practical and aesthetic motives, but the use of country sleighs persisted until the end of the Carriage Era. New designs included small, light cutters for one or two passengers and larger, more elegant sleighs that resembled vis-a-vis and barouche carriages on runners. Some carriages were designed with interchangeable wheels and runners, or bobs, for year-round use. Trade vehicles of all types, including large public conveyances such as the omnibus, were fitted with bobs for winter travel.

One of the most popular sleighs in America was the cutter, a light, one-horse sleigh with a single seatboard for two or three passengers. The best-known versions were the portland cutter and the albany cutter, both developed in the early nineteenth century. The albany cutter, made by James Goold of Albany, New York, was characterized by sweeping lines and a rounded, or swelled, body. Perhaps because of the expense of steam bending the side panels, fewer of these were sold by the end of the century. The portland cutter was developed in Portland, Maine, by Peter Kimball and his sons. It had more angular lines and flat body panels. This type was also called the kimball cutter, and many variations were produced by the Kimballs, some in cooperation with Brewster & Company in New York.

Most sleighs were ornamented, some with paint and striping and others with paintings or decals of animals and floral motifs. The enclosed sleighs of the late nineteenth century that were manufactured by established carriage makers exhibited craftsmanship equal to that of the finest private coaches, with luxurious interior trim and highly lustrous finishes. Passengers in all types of sleighs could keep warm with fur-trimmed clothing and the use of heated soapstones or footwarmers containing coal, charcoal or hot water. Additional warmth, especially in open sleighs, was provided by muffs and heavy lap robes of fur, wool or horsehair. The driver's hands were protected by special driving gloves, such as sealskin gloves that could be buckled to the reins.

The sound of sleigh bells announced the otherwise quiet passage of these vehicles on snowy roads. These included elegant terret or saddle bells that attached to the harness saddle and could be decorated with dyed horsehair plumes and shaft bells that were mounted directly on the sleigh shafts. Most commonly, however, a string of bells on a leather band was attached to the horse's belly or around its neck.

Sleighs of all types remained popular until the end of the Carriage Era. Included here are several country sleighs dating from 1770 to 1870, two variations of the swelled-body sleigh developed by Goold, a graceful cutter and a luxurious booby hut sleigh of the 1880s. Not included is The Museums livery stage on bobs.

The streets of our village have been enlivened during the past week with the jingle of a thousand merry sleigh bells. Every man who has a pair of runners has had them out during the past week—even the old crockery crate on bent hickory poles not being despised. The hearts of our village store keepers have been made glad by the customers who have come from a radius of a dozen miles in every direction. The falls of snow during the week have packed nicely, and give the promise of excellent sleighing for many days.

The Long Island Leader,
January 19, 1876

At Home in the Country: Winter *Not dated (c. 1865); Thomas Kelly, publisher; New York, New York; Museums collection*

54. Sleigh

Maker unknown, United States; c. 1770
98 × 58 × 39 in (249 × 147 × 99 cm)
Exterior, interior original; Museums
purchase, 1951

The heavy, box-like body of this early hand-crafted sleigh is painted dark green. The vehicle is equipped with fittings for as many as six seat boards. The front and rear panels are secured with a curved and jointed yoke to permit removal of the panels to convert the sleigh for hauling freight. The side panels could also be removed; these removable panels made the sleigh easier to store. The body is mounted on long runners and shaped, or saw-cut, knees, which are the vertical supports that connect the beams of the body to the runners.

This sleigh was owned by the American Revolutionary War hero Peter Gansevoort of Albany, New York. The initials "PG" are painted on the back panel.

55. Sleigh

Maker unknown, United States; c. 1820
84 × 60 × 60 in (213 × 152 × 152 cm)
Exterior, interior original; Museums
purchase, 1953

This two-passenger country sleigh is a rare survival; it represents the earliest efforts to construct sleigh bodies with steam-bent "swelled" panels, a design that came to be known as the albany cutter. The vertical panel ribs for support and the extended dash supported by the runners are also characteristic of early albany sleighs.

The curved vertical ribs lock into the upper frame with mortise and tenon joints. The armrests terminate in carved scrolls. The carved forward dash, which is separate from the body, is supported on graceful, vertical extensions of the front runner ends. Hand-wrought iron scrolls decorate the top of the dash and the back of the runners.

The body, painted yellow with black striping, has an exterior border of painted acanthus leaves along the upper edge of the panels. The chamfered wooden runner frame is ornamented with striping, which gives the effect of additional chamfering.

56. Sleigh

Maker unknown, United States; c. 1850
100 × 52 × 38 in (254 × 132 × 97 cm)
Exterior, interior original; Gift of Charles E.
Rockwell, 1973

Charles Embree Lawrence and friends in his sleigh, Smithtown, New York, c. 1912; Museums collection

The design, construction and ornamentation of this vehicle are typical of American country sleighs. The construction is heavier and less refined than in the streamlined, more refined sleighs that were mass-produced in the late nineteenth century, but it demonstrates the careful workmanship and fine artistry that were often employed in hand-crafted vehicles.

The sides have a gradual downward slope from the high backrest and curve upward again toward the rounded dash. The driver's seat, on scrolled ironwork, folds forward to admit passengers to the rear seats. The body is painted in two shades of yellow and decorated with an encircling border of leaves in two shades of green at the upper edge. The lower part of the panels is decorated with red and black striping in varying widths.

The yellow wooden runner frame has tapered knees. The iron runners terminate in hand-wrought closed curls at the front and back.

This sleigh was owned by Charles E. Lawrence of Smithtown, New York. It was used by his family until the early twentieth century and was donated to The Museums by his grandson.

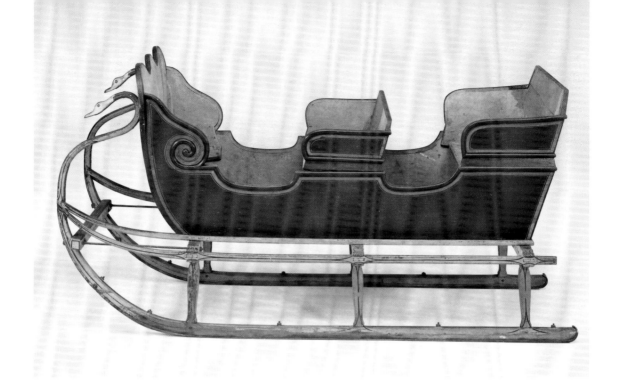

57. Sleigh

Maker unknown, United States; c. 1870
92 × 48 × 43 in (234 × 122 × 109 cm)
Exterior, interior original; Gift of Ward
Melville, 1971

The box-like body of this country sleigh is ornamented with a carved scroll design near the front of the side panels. The sleigh is painted brown with wide yellow striping. The middle seat is both reversible and removable and fittings are provided for an additional seat board close to the high dash. The knees are turned wood and the runners curve back toward the dash and terminate in gracefully-carved swans' heads.

58. Cutter

Brewster & Company, New York, New York
c. 1890; 58 × 51 × 38 in (147 × 130 × 97 cm)
Exterior, interior restored, probably 1951
Museums purchase, 1951

This variant of a portland cutter was made by Brewster & Company, which formed a limited partnership in 1876 with Charles P. Kimball, the son of Peter Kimball, who developed this popular sleigh design. It differs in a number of features from the typical portland or kimball design: for example, the front sides are extremely low or open and the side panels are slightly rounded instead of flat.

Leather snow guards follow the deep curve of the dash, which is ornamented with deep ironwork scrolls above the vertical rise of the runners. The scroll motif is repeated in the carved wooden ends of the seat back, the armrests and the gracefully curved ironwork runner frame that supports the body. The body is painted dark green-black and the seat trim is light green. A serial number 806 is in ink on a paper label on the seat.

59. Vis-a-Vis Sleigh

William Lown, Troy, New York; c. 1880
119 × 68 × 65 in (302 × 173 × 165 cm)
Exterior, interior restored 1953–1956; Gift of
Mrs. Fred Sickles, Mrs. Lila S. Churchill
and Mrs. Walter O. Noyes, Jr., in memory of
Frederick Sickles, 1953

The swelled body of this sleigh is typical of later versions of the albany sleighs. The name *vis-a-vis* derives from the seating arrangement, in which the passengers travel face-to-face.

The body is painted maroon with red striping and the trim is maroon broadcloth. Leather snow guards follow the curve of the dash, which is decorated with a pair of carved eagle heads. The runner frame has thin straight ironwork knees and is decorated with graceful curved ironwork at the front and the back.

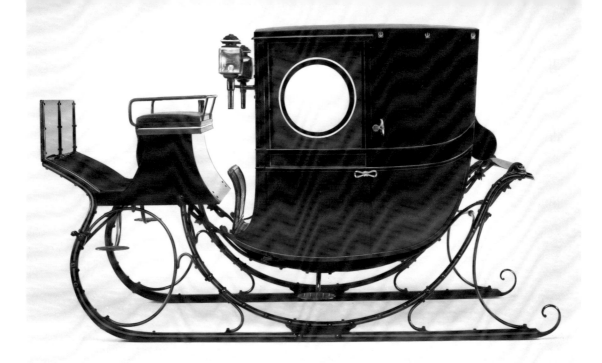

60. Booby Hut

J. T. Smith, Boston, Massachusetts; c. 1880
127 × 70 × 55 in (323 × 178 × 140 cm)
Exterior restored 1960; interior original
Gift of The Society for the Preservation of
New England Antiquities, Boston, Massachu-
setts, 1951

The term *booby hut* was used in New England to describe a sleigh with an enclosed body. The word *booby* was a pejorative term for an imbecilic or loutish person; this curiously negative name was applied, for unknown reasons, to an elegant and sometimes expensive vehicle.

The upper panels of the body of this sleigh are black; the lower panels and runners are painted maroon with vermillion striping. Three silver-plated wreath ornaments are applied to each side of the rear quarter panels. The door handles are in the shape of knotted bows and are silver-plated and decoratively incised. The round windows at the sides and the rear are beveled glass. Blond and dark wood stable shutters decoratively pierced with a wreath design are stored in slots beneath the windows. When the vehicle was in storage, these stable shutters could be pulled up to prevent sunlight or dust from damaging the trim.

A small ornamental sword case at the rear is accessible from the interior by folding down the hinged upper section of the rear passenger seat. The interior is beautifully trimmed in ribbed red velvet plush. The ceiling is covered with a pleated, figured red damask, with a rosette at the center. The window pulls, the broadlace and the holders are maroon and red silk woven in a geometric pattern. All are edged in a deep, twisted silk and wool fringe. The red silk curtains at each window have acorn-shaped tassels covered in red silk thread.

The interior is appointed with a mahogany calling-card case, a red velvet storage pouch and a folding child's seat. A flexible ball covered in net is attached to a silk-covered tube; when the ball is squeezed, it pneumatically operates the signal whistle under the coachman.

The body is hung on leather thoroughbraces suspended from the seat riser and the rear of the runner frame. The iron runner frame is gracefully curved to follow the lines of the body and is decorated with scrolled ironwork at the front and back.

Interior of the booby hut

FREIGHT AND TRADE VEHICLES

Before the mid-nineteenth century, American trade vehicles included both freight wagons for long-distance hauling and smaller delivery and service vehicles for use over shorter distances and in towns. Freight wagons pulled by two or more horses did most long-distance overland hauling before the mid-nineteenth century; the conestoga wagon, popularized in American literature and legend, was a large freight wagon pulled by six horses and used primarily in Maryland, Virginia, Pennsylvania and Ohio. The Museums collection includes a conestoga wagon, but it is, unfortunately, not in exhibitable condition. Few long-distance freight vehicles have survived, since they were rendered obsolete as early as the 1860s, when railroads linked both coasts of the country.

The growth of American industry and commerce, the improvement of roads and the diversity of American carriage manufacturing during the second half of the nineteenth century contributed to the development of new and specialized trade vehicles in both rural and urban areas. Light wagons were used by retail merchants to deliver meat, milk, dry goods, ice and other commodities to customers. Farmers used large market wagons to haul their produce to urban markets, and drays—heavy, stake-sided wagons without springs—were used to haul the heaviest loads of goods or construction materials. In highly populated urban areas, such specialized vehicles as horse-drawn street scrapers and street sprinklers were a familiar sight.

Trade vehicles became highly refined in construction and finishes, rivaling the quality of many vehicles used for personal transportation. Manufacturers of trade vehicles were ready and willing to customize commercial wagons according to customer specifications, and some trade vehicles were even built to resemble the product of a specific company. With the rise of advertising in America in the nineteenth century, businesses became aware of the advertising potential of the exterior panels of their vehicles and specified bold and colorful lettering, scrollwork, trademarks, slogans and even evocative scenes of historical, contemporary or product-related subjects.

Even after the railroads replaced horse-drawn vehicles for long-distance commerce, trade vehicles remained a vital link in the local distribution of goods and services from railway lines. The introduction of the automobile in the early twentieth century did not curtail the use of trade vehicles as abruptly as it did the use of personal carriages: trade vehicles were used well into the 1920s and 1930s, when gasoline-powered trucks became widely available.

This section includes a variety of retail trade wagons, from an 1870s peddler's wagon to vehicles that were used to sell or deliver meat, oil, perfumes and mail; there is even one example that made and dispensed popcorn. Not included here is The Museums grocery wagon. The Museums collection does not include an ice wagon: although ice wagons were among the most common trade vehicles during the Carriage Era, few are known to have survived.

St. Nicholas Hotel *1855; W. Stephenson & Co.,*
publisher; New York, New York; Photograph Courtesy
of the Museum of the City of New York

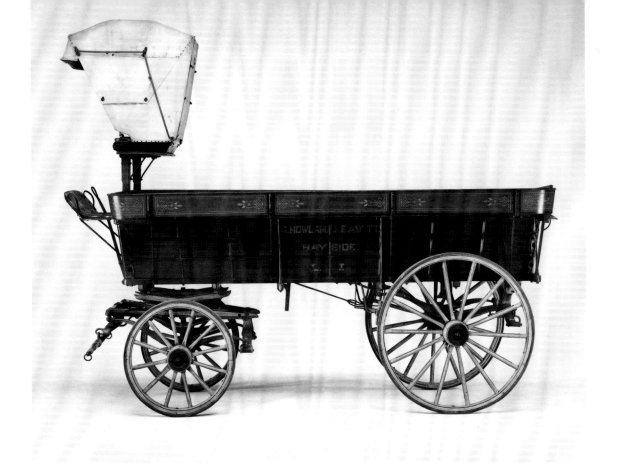

61. Market Wagon

Maker unknown, United States; c. 1900
134 × 146 × 71 in (340 × 371 × 180 cm)
Exterior, interior original; Gift of Mrs.
Henry Lewis III, Charles G. Meyer, Jr.,
G. Howland Meyer and S. Willets Meyer,
in memory of G. Howland Leavitt and
his daughter, Sara Willets Meyer, 1950

During the Carriage Era market wagons transported farm produce from rural to urban areas and manufactured goods from factories to local or distant markets. These journeys sometimes included transport of the vehicle itself on flatbed railroad cars or by ferry.

This example has a typically deep body, and the cargo space is increased by the ledges that overhang the wheels. The body is painted red and has chamfered, ribbed sides and a hinged door at the rear. The high driver's seat has a folding canvas hood; a foot brake runs from the rear axle up through the driver's footboard. The ledge panels, supported by metal rods, are decorated with multicolored stenciling.

The wagon is set on platform springs. The undercarriage is painted yellow with red and black striping. Produce would have been stacked as high as possible, covered with a tarp and secured by ropes.

This market wagon was originally owned by G. Howland Leavitt of Bayside, New York. It was donated to The Museums by four of his grandchildren.

62. Standard Oil Wagon

Maker unknown, United States; c. 1900
134 × 109 × 72 in (340 × 277 × 183 cm)
Exterior, interior original; Gift of B. Brewster Jennings for the Standard Oil Company, 1951

Oil delivery trucks were a common sight on American roads after the development of the petroleum industry in the nineteenth century. Such vehicles delivered kerosene for lamps and gear oil and grease to maintain farm equipment and other machinery. The Standard Oil Company, founded by John D. Rockefeller in Ohio in 1870, became the largest shipper of petroleum products in the nation. Its refineries were located near railroads to ensure the speedy transportation of its products; oil wagons carried those products from the railroad station to the customer. By 1900 Standard Oil operated more than 5,000 of these vehicles throughout the country. When automobiles were introduced, horse-drawn wagons like this one also delivered gasoline.

The large cylindrical metal tank holds approximately 350 gallons and is divided into two internal chambers. Petroleum and kerosene were loaded through hatches in the top and dispensed at the point of sale, through pipes at the rear, into containers provided by the customer. The body is painted green and carries the company name in shaded letters in white and yellow. The painted wooden storage box at the rear held five-gallon cans of axle grease and other lubricants. It is decorated with a star in metallic silver and orange paint.

The driver's seat is protected by a painted leather roof and side curtains. The body rests on a pair of bolster springs at the front and truck springs on the rear axle, where most of the weight was carried. The vehicle is equipped with a foot brake.

The oil wagon was donated to The Museums by Benjamin Brewster Jennings of New York for the Standard Oil Company. Mr. Jennings began working for the company in 1920; he served as president and chief executive officer from 1944 to 1958 and as a director of the company until his death in 1968.

63. Peddler's Wagon

Maker unknown, United States; c. 1865
117 × 81 × 68 in (297 × 206 × 173 cm)
Exterior, interior original; Museums
purchase, 1953

The traveling peddlers of early America were independent merchants who primarily sold imported goods. By the nineteenth century, they carried a wide variety of merchandise produced by American industries—rocking chairs, musical instruments, shoes, spectacles, pots and pans and bolts of cloth—and they often traded one object for another in lieu of a cash sale. Some of these peddlers later established store-based businesses that evolved into prominent American department stores, among them Abraham and Straus, Gimbel's and Sears, Roebuck and Company.

This peddler's wagon has a simple, rectangular body of planks, rather than the typically broad panels seen on most delivery wagons; it has a removable folding leather top. The body is painted off-white and carries the owner's name. The interior is lined with shelves; the roof rack and the boot below the driver's seat provided additional room for goods. The wooden crate attached to the rear of the vehicle is an egg carrying case marked "Fletcher's Patent Eggcase/S. T. Fletcher & Co./Sole Agents/ 114 So. Market St. Boston Mass.." One handle is stamped "Pat. Mar. 14 '82." The wagon is set on platform springs and the undercarriage is painted green with red and black striping.

This wagon originally belonged to L. L. Brown, of Hebron, New York, who used it between 1868 and 1880 to peddle eggs, groceries and other supplies to farms in the surrounding area. He later established a store and continued to use this wagon for making deliveries.

64. Butcher's Wagon

Maker unknown, United States; c. 1910
93 × 66 × 91 in (236 × 168 × 231 cm)
Exterior, interior original; Gift of Ward
Melville, 1971

Prior to the invention of electric refrigeration, meat was kept in icehouses or iceboxes. The butcher's wagon, a traveling shop, carried this meat to nearby neighborhoods. The driver made scheduled stops, where customers inspected the meat and the butcher cut and weighed it inside the wagon.

This example has a red panel-sided body. The sides and the bowed top are covered with white canvas. The rear canvas serves as an awning when the upper hinges are locked. The interior has shelves for meat, a wooden floor and a chopping block.

It is equipped with standard butcher tools: saws, cleavers, knives, a sharpening stone and a scale. The body is set on double-sweep elliptic springs. The gear is painted yellow with black striping.

This butcher's wagon belonged to K. J. Joslin, whose name appears on the driver's side panel. It was probably used in Vermont.

65. Mail Wagon

Hanford Wagon Works, Unadilla, New York
c. 1905; 76 × 72 × 45 in (193 × 183 × 114 cm)
Exterior, interior original; undercarriage
restored 1955; Museums purchase, 1953

Postal service in the United States began during the Carriage Era. Before rural free delivery, long-distance mail was carried on stage lines or by riders. Locally, patrons had to travel to sometimes distant post offices to send or receive mail. Experimentation with a postal delivery system began as early as 1863 in cities with populations of 20,000 or more, but rural free delivery was not established by the federal government until 1896. The postal department documented a twofold increase in letter writing, and rapidly expanded routes and established new postal districts.[1] Service was offered year-round, and sleighs were used during the winter months in the Northern states. Carriers were required to furnish and maintain their own vehicles, and many adapted their personal wagons and buggies for this work.

This mail wagon has a square metal body, painted green, with canvas sides and removable windows at the front and above the doors. The wood doors are painted green with black striping. The canvas roof is stretched over a lightly curved frame of wooden bows. The lower panels are decorated with decals of eagles and flags, and a flagpole socket is affixed to one of the lower front panels. Interior compartments carried letters and postal supplies, including stamps and envelopes. The rack at the rear carried larger parcels. When the front window was in place, the reins passed through two slots cut in the window frame. The vehicle is set on elliptic springs mounted parallel to the axle.

[1]Marshall Cushing, *The Story of Our Post Office* (Boston: A. M. Thayer & Co., 1893) 1013.

66. Tea Wagon

Biehle Wagon and Auto Body Works, Reading, Pennsylvania; c. 1910; 95 × 90 × 74 in (241 × 229 × 188 cm); Exterior, interior original; Museums purchase, 1955

The Eastern Estate Tea Company sold an exclusive line of merchandise that included tea, cocoa, spices, cereals, rice, maple syrup, peanut butter and soap products. With purchases, customers received premium trademarks that were redeemable for an assortment of household and personal objects.

The paneled and enclosed body of this wagon has an extension roof and the rear doors are fitted with oval windows. Painted canvas storm curtains could be attached at the driver's seat. The body is painted red and carries the company's name in bold gilt lettering around a large pagoda arch, the company's trademark, which also appeared on all its product packaging.

The vehicle is suspended on three elliptic springs, and the axles are connected by a reach. The undercarriage is yellow, accented with black freehand striping, which has an unusual waved pattern on the shoulders of the wheel spokes.

The Eastern Estate Tea Company was founded in the late 1880s by William E. Aiken, the original owner of this vehicle. The wagon was acquired from his family.

67. Popcorn Wagon

C. Cretors & Company, Chicago, Illinois
1907; 148 × 95 × 67 in (376 × 241 × 170 cm)
Exterior restored, some interior parts replaced
1956; Museums purchase, 1956

Modern popcorn wagons, developed during the early twentieth century, replaced the simple vendors' carts of earlier times, whose owners popped the corn manually over an open flame. The machinery for the popcorn popper and peanut roaster was driven by a gas or acetylene motor, whose gears and cogs were clearly visible to customers at amusement parks and parades. The fireproof body is made of steel and is decorated with colorful decals. It has beveled glass windows, chipped-glass signs and a retractable canvas awning. This wagon is equipped with a double popper, which

automatically buttered and salted the popcorn; the peanuts were automatically transferred to a warming tray after roasting.

The wagon is suspended on a pair of elliptic springs in the front and a pair of half-elliptic springs in the rear. The rear wheels are fitted with a braking mechanism that tightens leather bands around the hubs to keep the vehicle from rolling while business is conducted.

The manufacturer's 1913 catalog in The Museums Carriage Reference Library describes the benefits of owning one of

A view of the interior
equipment of the popcorn
wagon.

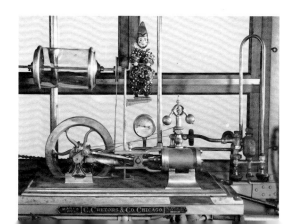

these popcorn wagons: "a business opportunity of exceptional value which combines all the pleasant elements of a legitimate, independent and lucrative occupation with a minimum investment." The firm of Charles Cretors & Company, although not vehicle builders, was famous for developing popcorn-making machines. This popcorn wagon, serial number 5157, was sold to Mr. A. W. Crosswell of Sumter, South Carolina for $1,350.[1]

[1]Charles D. Cretors, President, C. Cretors and Company, Letter to Laura Gombieski, May 7, 1986.

68. Perfume Wagon

Flynn & Doyle, Bantam, Connecticut; c. 1900
108×60×68 in (274×152×173 cm)
Exterior, interior restored 1952–1953
Museums purchase, 1952

This light specialty vehicle has numerous small, padded compartments to store and display bottles of perfume and extracts. The black, highly-varnished body carries the owner's business name in gold-leaf block lettering shaded in red. A fringed canopy top could be added to protect the driver's seat.

The vehicle is mounted on torsion springs, which consist of sidebar springs connected to the body above the rear axle and slightly behind the front axle by sets of wide, coiled steel bands. The wagon was owned and operated by Sterling Bunnell of Bristol, Connecticut, during the early twentieth century.

PUBLIC TRANSPORTATION

Several types of vehicles were used in America to carry mail and passengers overland and for short-distance travel in urban and rural areas. Hackney coaches were second hand coaches; by the early eighteenth century, they were available for hire in urban areas, as taxis are today. Stage lines, relatively few in number in colonial America, provided public transportation between major cities on the eastern seaboard. Stage traffic increased during the eighteenth century, especially after the Revolutionary War, as new roads were opened and existing roads were expanded. "By 1800, more than twenty-five separate stage lines were running out of Boston, and well over a hundred stages were arriving and departing each week."[1]

The establishment of overland mail routes and the westward expansion generated by the Gold Rush of 1849 increased the use of stages in all parts of the continent. Their use peaked during the second half of the nineteenth century, just as railroads were expanding from coast to coast. The first trains were, in fact, coaches hitched together and pulled along rails by a steam locomotive. Although railroads did replace stagecoach lines for long-distance travel, they did not diminish the need for horse-drawn transportation. Stages still served areas without rail service, and railroad traffic actually increased the need for local horse-drawn travel to and from railway stations. Even after the introduction of the automobile, stage lines continued to serve very remote areas into the 1920s.

The earliest public stages for long-distance travel were box-like, open wagons with bench seats. Fixed roofs and side curtains were soon added to protect the passengers from inclement weather. During the first quarter of the nineteenth century, however, an increasing number of American stages were constructed with enclosed bodies—oval or rounded in profile—similar to some European coaches. Some evidence exists to indicate that these early American stagecoaches were developed by Eaton & Gilbert and other coach makers in Troy, New York; a similar vehicle originally built in 1827 in Concord, New Hampshire, became the concord coach, the symbol of American overland travel during the nineteenth and the early twentieth centuries. The first concord coach was built by J. Stephens Abbot, an employee and later a partner of Lewis Downing.

The Abbot-Downing Company became the preeminent builder of overland stagecoaches. Unlike other carriage builders, the company continued to use earlier production methods, constructing their vehicles almost entirely by hand. Instead of steel springs, they used heavy leather thoroughbraces, like those used during the previous centuries. This sturdy suspension system was well suited to travel on rugged terrain, and spare braces could easily be carried to make repairs if the vehicle broke down in a remote area. The strength, durability and comfort of concord coaches established the company's reputation throughout the United States and abroad, and their overland vehicles were exported to Africa, South America and Australia.

During the nineteenth and early twentieth centuries a number of smaller and lighter coaches and wagons were used to transport passengers over shorter distances in rural and suburban areas. Road coaches and mail coaches were similar to the concord coach. Wagons, called overland wagons, western or california wagons and mud wagons were just a few of the types that became known in the West and other

The Saratoga Depot—Arrival of the Train;
Frank Leslie's Illustrated Newspaper; *August 16,
1873; Collection of George S. Bolster; Photograph
Courtesy of the Historical Society of Saratoga
Springs, New York*

areas of the country. In resort areas both
hotels and livery establishments operated
these vehicles to transport their customers to
and from railway stations. Various styles of
wagonettes became known as depot wagons,
station wagons or station omnibuses.
Mountain wagons were used for excursions
in rugged terrain and some livery companies
in resort areas operated large omnibuses that
could carry 12 to 40 passengers on sightsee-
ing tours.

In urban areas a variety of vehicles was
developed to serve the short-distance transportation needs of a growing American
population. These included the hackney

coach, the cab and the omnibus. These
street vehicles were American adaptations of
vehicles popular in Europe during the
eighteenth century.

The vehicle developed for public transportation of large numbers of people was
called the omnibus. A prototype of this
vehicle was first introduced in Paris in 1662
for the private use of wealthy aristocrats. In
1819 Jacques Lafitte introduced an omnibus
in Paris that was built by George Shillibeer,
an English coach maker working in France.
After Shillibeer returned home he introduced the omnibus to England in 1829.

The first such vehicle in the United
States, named the "Accommodation," was
built by the firm of Wade & Leverich for
Abraham Brower of New York City in 1827.
This open, low-sided vehicle had a fixed
roof on pillars, a side entrance and seats

placed crosswise. Two years later Brower introduced the "Sociable," which had a rear entrance and knifeboard seats placed longitudinally. The first vehicle that was actually called an omnibus in the United States was built by John Stephenson of New York in 1831. The American omnibus was mounted on elliptic springs or thoroughbraces and, later, like its English counterparts, was often fitted with windows or roll-up curtains and spiral staircases for access to additional seats on the roof. The side panels were gaily decorated and carried signs describing the vehicle's route and the advertisements of local businesses.

Stephenson's company also built horse cars, large box-like omnibuses pulled by horses along fixed rails in the street. Designed for 12 to 40 passengers, horse cars were popular in many American and European cities until they were replaced by electric trolleys in the late nineteenth and early twentieth centuries.

Other types of public transportation vehicles in urban areas were the two-wheel hackney cab and the hansom cab, both used in Europe as well as in the United States during the nineteenth century. The term *cab*, a shortened derivation from the name of the owner-driven cabriolet (see Cat. No. 47), was combined with the term *hackney* to denote a vehicle for hire. The hansom cab was designed by the English architect Joseph A. Hansom in 1834 and improved by John Chapman a few years later. It differs from the cabriolet in that it has a much lower body, for ease of access, and the coachman's seat is perched high on the roof. Both vehicles provided a welcome alternative for those who could afford to pay a higher fare for the increased speed and privacy not found in the public omnibuses, which travelled set routes and accommodated a large number of people. The hansom cab, already popular in Europe by the mid-nineteenth century, did not see frequent use in the United States until late in the century, and then most commonly in New York City.

Of The Museums public transportation vehicles, five of the eight included here were made by the Abbot-Downing Company. They represent a variety of vehicles used for overland and mountain travel, for short-distance stage lines in rural areas and for local travel in resort areas during the nineteenth and early twentieth centuries. An omnibus made for a livery company on the coast of Maine, is the largest and most elaborately decorated vehicle in The Museums collection. Also shown in this chapter are an English-made hansom cab and a rural depot wagon of Long Island manufacture.

---

[1]Oliver W. Holmes, and Peter T. Rohrbach, *Stagecoach East* (Washington, D.C.: Smithsonian Institution Press, 1983) 34.

69. Wells Fargo Coach

Abbot-Downing Company, Concord, New Hampshire; c. 1870; 163 × 105 × 75 in (414 × 267 × 191 cm); Exterior, interior original; canvas curtains restored 1960; Gift of the Railway Express Agency, 1959

The Wells Fargo Overland Express Company figured prominently in America's westward expansion. The company provided coach transportation for passengers and mail and operated banking offices throughout the West. During the mining boom of the mid-nineteenth century, its coaches transported millions of dollars' worth of gold bullion and exchanged it for money at the banking offices. Wells Fargo was one of the 400 western express companies that carried the country's mail from 1848 until 1896, when the federal government took over that function. Passengers rode in the company's coaches from the Midwest to the West on a number of overland trails.

This rugged vehicle is suspended with thoroughbraces. Unlike the fancier stage and hotel coaches made by the Abbot-Downing Company, this vehicle, a heavy type of mud wagon, is devoid of decoration and luxury appointments. The body is painted the standard Wells Fargo red and the undercarriage is yellow. The interior trim and curtains are of plain, heavy canvas. Luggage was carried in the rear boot and valuable cargo, such as strongboxes containing gold and mail, was stored in the boot under the driver's seat. Each Wells Fargo coach could accommodate nine passengers inside and six to ten on the roof, which was fitted with a handrail for support.

This vehicle was in use until 1906. It was exhibited by the Railway Express Agency until 1951.

70. Concord Coach

Abbot-Downing Company, Concord,
New Hampshire; c. 1875; 162 × 104 × 78 in
(411 × 264 × 198 cm); Exterior, interior
original; Gift of Webster Knight II, 1962

The large, ovoid, curved panel body of this vehicle is typical of the concord coach, as are the wrought-iron hardware and the use of leather thoroughbraces for suspension. The door panels feature oval paintings: the scene on the left is a seascape with a lighthouse and a sailing vessel, while the scene on the right depicts a coach under attack by Indians. Eagles are painted on the box seat panels, and the upper panels are painted with the words "Mattapoisett and New Bedford/C. E. Fuller."

The interior is trimmed in a deep red cut velvet in a floral design. The ceiling and swags are maroon and gold damask in a morning-glory pattern and are edged in a twisted wool fringe. The seaming and pasting lace is red and blue; the broadlace is a geometric pattern in white, red, yellow and blue. The serial number is 124.

Charles E. Fuller was a stage driver from 1865 to 1882 and worked for the Fall River stage line and Paulding's Express, both based in New Bedford, Massachusetts. Between 1883 and 1901 he was the proprietor of the Mattapoisett stage line, New Bedford.

Interior of the concord coach

71. Coach

Abbot-Downing Company; Concord, New Hampshire; c. 1880; 165 × 105 × 84 in (419 × 267 × 213 cm.); Exterior and interior original; Museums purchase, 1953

This hotel coach is a fine example of Abbot-Downing craftsmanship in construction, painting and trim. The dark red body has shaded gold-leaf lettering and striping. Hand-painted landscapes on the door panels depict the Crawford House surrounded by mountains on one door, and the road leading to the resort hotel on the other. The interior trim is green leather and red velvet trimmed with a floral patterned broadlace. The ceiling is edged with green, yellow and red silk tassels; the painted canvas curtains are edged in figured silk damask. The body is hung on rugged leather thoroughbraces. The serial number 186 is stamped on the hubcaps.

The coach holds 24 passengers, 12 inside and 12 on the roof. Luggage was carried on the rear cradle; when the coach was filled with passengers, a separate vehicle for luggage accompanied it. This coach was one of the vehicles used by the Crawford House in Crawford Notch, New Hampshire, one of the first hotels to accommodate vacationers in the White Mountains, and an elegant summer resort by the 1880s.

The vehicle was used to transport hotel guests to and from distant railway stations over narrow mountain roads, and for excursions to scenic areas. It was also used to convey passengers to the annual summer coaching parades that were held in nearby towns. These colorful parades drew participants from many mountain resorts and were considered the highlight of the summer season. After the end of the Carriage Era this coach was used for special occasions at the Crawford House until 1953.

Interior of the coach used at Crawford House

72. Mountain Wagon

Abbot-Downing Company, Concord,
New Hampshire; c. 1880; 148 × 79 × 78 in
(376 × 201 × 198 cm.); Exterior, interior
original; Museums purchase, 1953

Mountain wagons were excursion vehicles used to transport passengers into rugged scenic areas in many parts of the United States. This example was used in Crawford Notch, New Hampshire, for visitors to the Crawford House resort.

The box-shaped body has ribbed sides. The seats are transverse and the third seat is hinged to fold forward. The body is painted vermillion and striped in black and yellow. "Crawford House" is painted in gold-leaf block letters on the sides; "Mount Willard," also in gold leaf, is painted on both sides of the seat riser. The names "Barron &

Merrill," obscured by darkened varnish, are painted on the sides of the seat riser. Barron and Merrill owned the Crawford House and two other nearby resorts in the White Mountains of New Hampshire.

The body is suspended on heavy leather thoroughbraces and the undercarriage is painted yellow with black striping. A step attached to the brake applies the entering passenger's weight to the brake to prevent the vehicle from rolling. The brake can also be operated by a lever from the driver's seat.

73. Hack Passenger Wagon

Abbot-Downing Company, Concord,
New Hampshire; 1862–1870; 125 × 94 × 79
in (318 × 239 × 201 cm); Exterior, interior
original; Museums purchase, 1958

The hack passenger wagon was Abbot-Downing's smaller and less embellished version of the late-nineteenth-century public transportation vehicles used for short-distance travel in rural areas. The vehicle is characterized by a square body and seating for four to six passengers.

This example appears to be a four-passenger vehicle. It includes a luggage rail on the roof, a luggage rack on the rear, glass windows that slide into the door panels and side curtains at the windows. The body and undercarriage are painted yellow and there are modest scrollwork paintings on the doors.

The interior ceiling and sides are trimmed in gold wool and a figured silk damask edged in fringe. The body is hung on thoroughbraces. Its serial number is 411.

This vehicle was driven by the Civil War veteran Joel Chase Pierce on a scheduled route between Waldoboro, Maine, on the coast, to Washington and Liberty, Maine. The faded letters over the doors read "R. C. Moores," probably for Robert C. Moores, the owner of a stage line in Washington, Maine.

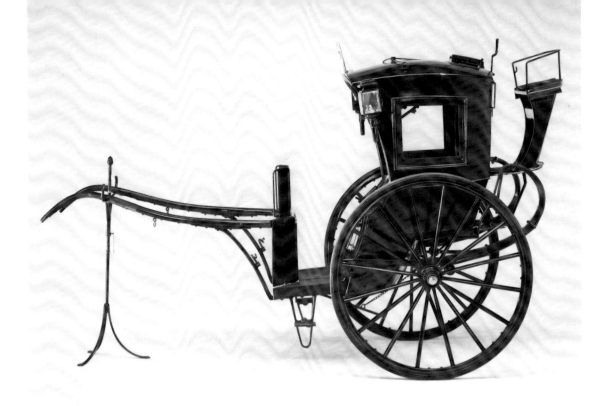

74. Hansom Cab

Forder & Company, London, England;
c. 1890; 155 × 74 × 94 in
(394 × 188 × 239 cm); Exterior restored
1953; interior original Gift of Ward Melville,
1971

The first hansom cab had extremely high wheels and a driver's seat mounted on the roof. In 1836 Englishman John Chapman improved the original design by lowering the wheels and mounting the driver's seat at the rear of the cab. Further improvements by the carriage manufacturer Forder & Company included the use of better materials in manufacture, safety features, reduced weight and a more comfortable interior—and won prizes from the British carriage industry.

The high driver's seat allows a clear view of the horses and traffic. The reins run through a bracket mounted on the roof. A lever in front of the driver's seat operates the chain crank mechanism that opens and closes the doors. Cab fare was collected through a small trapdoor in the ceiling of the passenger compartment. The body is painted black. The serial number 5237 is on both ends of the axle and on the brass toe rail.

The interior, trimmed in black leather, is fitted with glass windows, which can be lowered in bad weather. The vehicle is hung on C-springs and has a high curved leather splashboard. When it is not in use, its weight rests on the V-shaped iron braces of the step plates and the metal stem centered under the body.

75. Station Omnibus

George E. Gould, Lake Grove, New York;
1906; 122 × 66 × 90 in (310 × 168 × 229 cm)
Exterior, interior restored 1978; Gift of
Mrs. Gilbert Brunelli, 1951

This enclosed wagonette has low panel sides and turned spindles to support the seat rail. The fixed roof, supported on slender pillars, extends over the driver's seat. A private omnibus would have been fitted with glass windows; a public omnibus like this one would have had canvas or leather side curtains.

The vehicle has knifeboard seats. Access is through a rear door by the use of a step plate. The vehicle is suspended on platform springs.

This omnibus was built for Samuel A. Hawkins of Stony Brook, New York. It was used to transport passengers between the Stony Brook railroad station and the village of Setauket. A separate wagon would have carried the passengers' luggage.

The Stony Brook station
omnibus with passengers,
Old Field Lighthouse,
Old Field, Setauket,
New York, c. 1915;
Museums collection

76. Omnibus

Concord Carriage Builders, Concord,
New Hampshire; c. 1880; 276 × 132 × 96 in
(701 × 335 × 244 cm); Exterior, interior
original; conserved 1984–1986; Gift of St.
Paul's School, Concord, New Hampshire,
1952

This type of large omnibus, sometimes called a "barge," was used primarily in New England for excursions. Many of these vehicles were named for famous persons or locations; this omnibus is named "Grace Darling" after a popular maritime heroine who was responsible for the dramatic rescue of survivors from a shipwreck off the coast of England in 1838.

The lower body is concave and rises to a ledge, which increases the interior space. The corners of the body are rounded. Above the ledge is a shallow rail supported by turned spindles. A wide seat rail is attached to the fixed pillars that support the roof. The curved roof has an iron luggage rail around the edge. The door and steps are located at the rear.

The body is painted red. The sides of the roof are painted with the words "S. P. Huntress. South Berwick, ME." The sides of the body carry the name "Grace Darling" in gold-leaf letters blocked in two shades of blue. The seat rails and pillars are straw-colored and are decorated with red and blue striping and geometric designs. The spindles are painted yellow and black. The corners of the body have painted medallions that feature a stag, a falcon, fruit and flowers. The curved underside of the toeboard is decorated with a swag and shield in shaded gold leaf. The seat risers have circular portraits of female figures. The door panel carries rectangular paintings that include a stag, a dog and a mid-nineteenth-century Diana-like figure with a bow and quiver—emblematic of the name of the owner, Huntress.

The interior is fitted with knifeboard wooden seats and straps for storm curtains. The lower edge of the roof interior is painted straw color and has twelve oval landscapes of extraordinary quality, each surrounded by a gray Eastlake-style border. These interior panels are believed to have been painted by John Burgum (1826–1907), an easel painter who also worked as the chief ornamenter for the Abbot-Downing Company of Concord.

The vehicle was drawn by two or four horses. It is suspended on platform springs, and the undercarriage is painted light yellow with red and blue striping.

This omnibus was operated by the Huntress family, owners of a livery business in South Berwick, Maine, from the 1860s to 1904. It was acquired by St. Paul's School in Concord, New Hampshire, in 1925 and was used to transport athletic teams to sporting events until 1952.

Interior of the omnibus
"Grace Darling"

FIRE-FIGHTING VEHICLES

Among the specialized vehicles of the Carriage Era were those used for fire fighting. The threat of fire was constant, terrifying and very real; most buildings were highly flammable, and heat and light were generally provided by some sort of open flame. Before the early nineteenth century, fires were fought by lines of men passing water-filled buckets from the water source—well, pump, river or lake—to the fire. From the eighteenth century, the efforts of firemen were assisted by "engines," machines for pumping water that enabled a longer and greater throw of water onto the flames. The earliest of these hand-operated water pumpers, which were made primarily of wood, were developed in Europe during the seventeenth century and were used in urban centers in the United States by the early eighteenth century. Volunteer firemen pulled the pumper to a fire, where water was supplied to the engine by a bucket brigade. The pumper, manually operated by firemen, shot the water to the flames in spurts.

Improvements in engines to enable them to deliver a steady stream of water were made in England during the first quarter of the eighteenth century, and the new pumpers were quickly imported for use in major American cities. These were operated by bar levers on either side of a box-like pump on wheels. A row of men on each side alternately depressed and raised the levers to pump the water, which was still supplied to the pumper by bucket brigades. Improvements in the construction of leather hoses were made in the first decades of the nineteenth century, providing firemen access to more distant sources of water without the use of bucket brigades. These long water hoses were transported to fires on hose carriages. Usually, a separate volunteer fire company pulled and operated the pumper and another company pulled the hose carriages and directed the water from the hoses to the fire.

The steam pumper, first developed in the 1840s, utilized the power of a steam engine instead of manpower to pump water from its source to a fire. These powerful engines, made mostly of metal, were so extremely heavy that they had to be pulled by horses rather than men. Although the steam pumper was a vastly more efficient fire-fighting tool than the hand pumper, it was viewed with suspicion by most volunteer fire companies, at least partly because relatively few men were needed to operate it compared to the dozens required to man a hand pumper. After the middle of the nineteenth century, when major cities began to replace volunteer fire companies with paid fire departments, steam pumpers quickly replaced hand pumpers. Volunteer fire departments remained active only in smaller towns and rural areas and they, too, eventually changed from hand pumpers to steam pumpers. Volunteer fire companies continued to play—as they do today—a vital role in many American communities, fighting fires and serving as local civic organizations with great pride in their equipment, their fraternal membership and their praiseworthy accomplishments in fighting fires.

Included in this section are four of The Museums fire-fighting vehicles: an early-nineteenth-century hand pumper; two hose carriages, with one example made for parade use; and an 1874 steam pumper, the heaviest vehicle in The Museums collection.

77. Side-Stroke Gooseneck Pumper

Maker unknown, probably United States
1810–1830; 190 × 81 × 55 in
(483 × 206 × 140 cm); Exterior original
Museums purchase, 1959

Fire-fighting engines in the American colonies were initially imported from England. By the mid-eighteenth century, American manufacturers were producing manually operated pumpers, called "engines," like this example of the popular gooseneck pumper. The name derives from the shape of the pipe that rises from the condensing case. The pipe was mounted so it could rotate; when coupled with fire hose,

it provided great flexibility and accuracy in delivering a stream of water onto a fire. Water pressure was built within the condensing case by pumping the levers, or "brakes," on the sides of the engine.

The box-like body has recessed paneling and is painted in a technique that simulates wood grain. A signature on the engine reads "Val. R. Krapp, Painter." The rectangular condensing case above the body has a convex back with small Doric columns on either side. "College Point/Exempt/1807" is painted on the back in gold-leaf block letters. The sides of the case are decorated with gilded metal reliefs of fruit and flowers. The body is mounted directly on the running gear; the hubs are rimmed with brass bands.

This vehicle would have been hand-drawn to a fire and operated by volunteer firemen. The apparatus is believed to have been first used by a volunteer fire company in Manhattan. It was purchased in 1857 for Union Engine Company No. 1 of College Point, Queens County, New York, where it was used until 1878.

78. Hose Carriage

Maker unknown, United States; c. 1870
138 × 66 × 138 in (351 × 168 × 351 cm)
Restored, probably 1952; Gift of the
Association of Exempt Firemen, Patchogue,
New York, 1951

Because fire engines were rarely equipped to carry long lengths of hose, hand-drawn or horse-drawn hose carriages were an indispensable part of fire fighting in the nineteenth century. Hose was laid from the water supply to the pumper and from the pumper to the flames. Firemen preferred riveted leather hose because of its flexibility and strength, and the heavy weight of this hose required a means of transport that was light and maneuverable. Four-wheel hose carriages like this example were known as the "spider" type; two-wheel hose carriages were called "jumpers."

The large reel of this vehicle carried up to 900 feet of hose. The circular metal frames on each side of the reel cylinder are painted red with gold and black striping. The glass on the lamps is decorated with paintings depicting a bird, flowers, a fireman, a burning building and the number "1." Two oil torches are mounted at the rear. "Exempt Firemen of Patchogue" is painted on the sides of the frame and "Patchogue, N.Y." is stamped on the metal seat back.

The hose carriage is suspended on elliptic and scroll-end springs. It was used by the fire department of Patchogue, New York, from approximately 1870 to 1904.

79. Steam Pumper

Amoskeag Manufacturing Company, Manchester, New Hampshire; 1874
158 × 115 × 80 in (401 × 292 × 203 cm)
Restored prior to 1960; Museums purchase, 1962

The body and fittings of this horse-drawn steam pumper are made of brass, copper, nickel and plated metal. The corners of the wooden firebox at the rear are decorated with paintings of hunting dogs and birds as well as the engine's name, "T. J. Coolidge," in block lettering. The undercarriage is red with white, gold and blue striping and gold-leaf scrollwork.

The pumper was originally built for the fire department of New Orleans, Louisiana. Because of its extreme weight—9,240 pounds—and immense size, the apparatus proved to be too large to maneuver easily on that city's narrow streets. It was returned to the manufacturer, who used it for fighting fires at the factory and in the town of Manchester, New Hampshire. The pumper was named after Thomas Jefferson Coolidge, president of the Board of Direc-

tors of the Amoskeag Manufacturing Company and a great-grandson of Thomas Jefferson. Most pumpers the size of this one were drawn by three horses pulling abreast. This engine was capable of pumping nine hundred gallons of water per minute. The Amoskeag Manufacturing Company, one of the most prominent manufacturers of steam fire engines, was a division of the Manchester Locomotive Works.

Running to a Fire in New York *February 24, 1972; Thomas Worth;* **Harper's Weekly;** *Museums collection*

80. Parade Hose Carriage

Rumsey Manufacturing Company, Seneca Falls, New York; 1875; 132 × 120 × 68 in (335 × 305 × 173 cm); Partially restored 1960–1961; Museums purchase, 1962

During civic celebrations, firemen displayed their equipment and vied for awards. The pride that individual fire companies took in their equipment often led them to make elaborate additions to or adaptations of basic vehicles specifically for the purpose of parading, and many manufacturers of fire-fighting apparatus offered parade options such as removable decorative attachments.

This hand-drawn hose carriage is resplendent with silver plating from its axles and springs to the removable statue and vases mounted on top. The hose drum is decorated with etched glass mirrors in a sunburst pattern and the ends of the drum are ornamented with scallop shells containing statuettes of classical figures. A pair of brass dragons on top support silver-plated vases that would have held fresh-cut flowers when the vehicle was on parade. Originally the hose carriage had seven cut-glass lamps, five of which are still extant. A pair of silver-plated bells hangs between the front lamps and a brass eagle mounted on a sphere is affixed between the rear lamps. Crowning the very top is a silver-plated statue of winged Cupid holding a bow and quiver. Inscribed at the base of the statue is "J. Coutan. Rome. 1875." The oblong wooden toolboxes over the axles are framed with silver-plated bands and are decorated with brass figures of a griffin and Columbia. A reel mounted forward of the front axle carried the drag line or rope that enabled the firemen to pull the vehicle. The carriage is mounted on elliptic springs.

This hose carriage was owned by Ringgold Hose Company #1 of Newburgh, New York. The vehicle cost approximately $2,000; the funds to purchase it were probably raised by community donations. The hose carriage would have been used for both fire fighting and parading.

Major Parts of a Vehicle

1 joint
2 prop nut
3 curtain light
4 back curtain
5 seat
6 seat riser
7 boot
8 body
9 reach
10 rub iron
11 step
12 axle nut
13 hub
14 spoke
15 felloe
16 tire
17 dash

18 dash rail
19 seat cushion fall
20 cushion
21 bow
22 socket

1 door panel
2 step
3 upper quarter panel
4 lower quarter panel
5 lamps
6 boot
7 arch panel
8 footboard
9 dash
10 seat-fall
11 driving cushion
12 pump handle
13 squab
14 holder

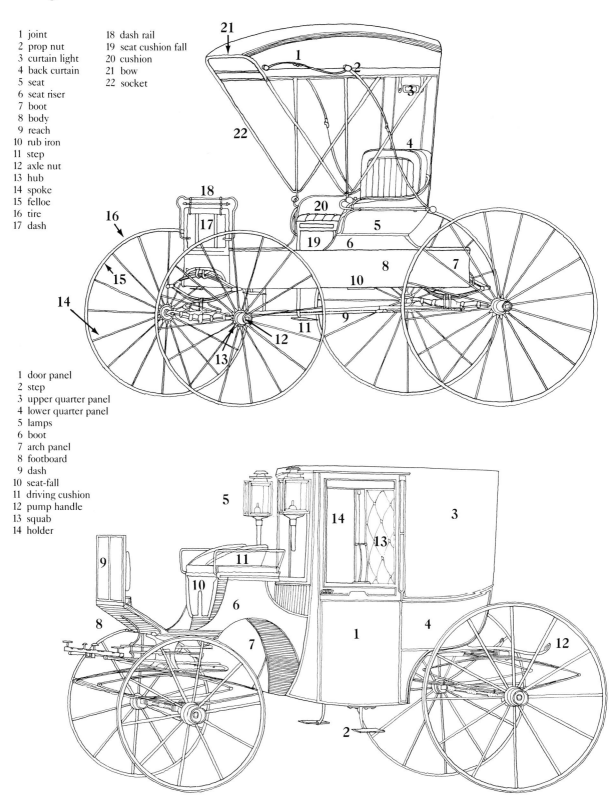

The illustrations on this page and page 123 by Victor Lazarro are derived from diagrams in various publications in The Museums Carriage Reference Library.

Springs

C-spring

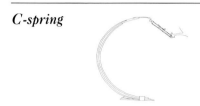

Developed c. 1790. An improvement of the whip spring. Metal plates curved in the shape of a C and attached to the body at the top ends by leather braces.

Double-elbow

Date of origin uncertain; in general use by 1780. Also called *Grasshopper, Side, Cross* and *Half-elliptic.* Two elbow springs joined at the center, curving slightly at the ends, where they are attached, or shackled, to the underside of the body. Usually used in combination with other springs. While similar in form, *Side* springs were positioned perpendicular to the axle and *Cross* springs were parallel to the axle.

Elliptic Spring

Elliptic   *Double-sweep Elliptic*

Developed c. 1802. A pair of curved metal leaf springs bolted or shackled together at the ends to form an ellipse. Although there is evidence that elliptic springs were used prior to 1802, Obadiah Elliot's patent in that year involved the novel use of elliptic springs without a perch.

Double-sweep Elliptic springs are nearly identical to elliptic, but flatten to a greater degree toward the ends where the upper and lower sections of the spring are connected.

Half-elliptic springs are only one-half of a full elliptic spring.

Platform Springs

Date of origin uncertain. A combination spring consisting of two side springs joined by a cross spring, generally used on heavier vehicles. They were sometimes employed only over the rear axle, with a pair of elliptic springs at the front.

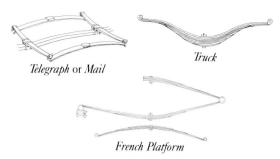

Telegraph or *Mail*   *Truck*

French Platform

Telegraph or *Mail* springs are a type of platform spring, being a combination of two side and two cross springs arranged in a square. They were first used on the English stage coach "Telegraph" in 1826, and were employed on heavy vehicles such as the mail coach.

French Platform springs, used only on the rear axle, resemble a three-quarter elliptic, connected by a cross spring below and attached to the body above.

Truck springs, considered a type of platform spring, are heavy half-elliptic springs lacking the cross spring. They were used on trucks and other freight vehicles.

Scroll Spring

Date of origin uncertain. A spring bent at one end or both ends in the shape of a scroll.

Side-Bar Springs

Developed c. 1850. A type of wooden side spring that consists of two resilient wooden bars running parallel along either side of the body, connected to the body at either end by half-elliptic springs. Among the most successful patented side-bar springs was J. B. Brewster's of 1873, which also incorporated cross springs clipped to the side bars passing beneath the body.

Whip-Spring

Developed c. 1700. An early form of spring consisting of several overlapping metal plates, or leaves, bent in a slight curve. The springs are attached to the body at the top ends by leather braces, suspending the body above the undercarriage.

Glossary

Axle: a fixed transverse bar of metal or wood connecting wheels that revolve around the ends of the bar.

Bobs: short sleds, joined together and usually faced in iron, on which a sleigh rides or slides along snow or ice. The front unit turns around a king bolt and is sometimes affixed to a fifth wheel.

Bolster: a wood support connecting the axle to the underside of the body of a heavy wagon that is without springs.

Boot, or budget: a container or compartment for storing luggage and tools. On early coaches some were made of basketwork; later versions were wooden boxes with leather lids. In many pleasure-driving vehicles the hind boot is eliminated and the front boot is cut down to form a support for the driver's seat, which may also be called a boot.

Bows: narrow strips of wood bent or bowed at two points to form a support for a carriage top or a canvas wagon cover.

Brace: a strap, generally made of leather, used as a means of arresting the vehicle's motion (*check-strap*), or as a means of suspending a vehicle (*thorough-brace*); a part that lends support to another part.

Brake block, or **brake shoe:** a wooden or iron block, operated by a lever from the driver's seat, that applies friction or braking pressure to a wheel to slow a vehicle.

Broadlace: a woven textile strap or wide band, usually ornamental, used for trimming cushion fronts, borders, and holders inside carriages.

Budget: see *boot*.

Cane work: woven reeds or caning used to create an ornamental panel or light, open framework, such as is applied to the framing of chair seats; imitation or "sham" caning was achieved through either painting or mechanical wood carving and was used on exterior quarter panels.

Chamfered: furrowed or beveled, as the edges on woodwork.

Check strap: a leather strap connecting the sides of a carriage body to the perch, used to prevent excessive motion of the vehicle.

Cradle: a framework of wooden bars and rods, like a rack, to hold luggage at the back of public transportation vehicles such as coaches.

Crossbar: (1) any piece of wood placed transversely in a carriage body or gear; (2) on a one-horse vehicle, the piece fixed between the shafts on which the whiffletree is pivoted.

Curtain: leather or cloth drapery to enclose carriage windows. On coaches or country vehicles these are sometimes mounted on the exterior; most carriages have interior curtains. In finer carriages the curtains may be made of silk and fitted with a mechanism for storage and use, as in roll-up curtains.

Cut-under: cut away, as the portion of the body of a vehicle that is eliminated to allow the front wheels to pass under without striking the body. A *full lock* occurs when the wheels can turn completely under the body without restriction.

Dash: an upright frame or small panel, made of wood, iron or metal mesh, fixed to the front of a vehicle to deflect the mud and water thrown up by the horses' feet; a *dash rail* is the metal railing around or on the upper edge of a dash.

Drag shoe: an iron block or a box, attached by a chain, that is manually applied under a wheel as an additional braking mechanism on downgrades.

Felloes: the curved wooden segments that form the rim of a wheel and are held in place by the outer metal rim.

Fifth wheel: two circular or semi-circular iron plates connecting the underside of the front of the body to the front axle. The plates, which are usually greased to facilitate movement, revolve against each other, enabling the axle to turn.

Footman: a servant who accompanied a vehicle, employed usually on formal vehicles; the footman occupied a seat beside the driver, or a seat at the rear of the vehicle, sometimes called the *footman's standard* or *pageboard*.

Footplate: see *steps*.

Four-in-hand: the sport of driving four horses holding the reins all in one hand.

Gear: the under part of a vehicle, comprised of functioning parts (springs, wheels, axles) as distinct from the body; also called the *undercarriage*.

Glass string: or *glass frame lifter:* a strip of broadlace or leather attached to the window frame, by which it is raised or lowered in the bed in the door or body.

Groom: a stable servant who was responsible for grooming horses and performing other tasks in preparing and maintaining horses. Also a servant whose function was identical with that of the footman.

Hammercloth: ornamental valance on the coachman's seat on formal or state vehicles, often embellished with lace, gimp, fringe and tassels.

Head leather: the leather forming the hood of a vehicle.

Holder: a loop of broadlace, cloth or leather attached to the inside of the door pillars; it was used as a handle by passengers to assist in their entry into or exit from a vehicle.

Hub: the central part of a wheel that fits over the ends of the axle. *Hubcaps* are removable caps that fit over the ends of the axles; *hub bands* are metal bands that encircle the hub of a wheel to reinforce the wood; *hub nuts* are large nuts used to secure the wheels to the threaded axle ends.

Kingpin or **king bolt:** the bolt connecting the front axle to the rest of the carriage and the pivot upon which the axle turns. A *snipebill* is a primitive kingpin made of two interlocking eyebolts.

Knee apron: a piece of leather or rubberized cloth, often lined with wool or other material, that is attached at one end to the dash and can be unrolled to protect the front seat occupants' knees.

Knees: upright members, usually of wood, that connect a sleigh's runners to its body.

Lace: woven ornamental or plain web with a loop surface used in carriage trimming; *pasting lace,* narrow and with one edge unornamented, was used as a finishing edge or decorative border; *seaming lace,* also narrow, was used to cover cords. See also *broadlace.*

Lazy back: a light and temporary, sometimes padded backrest that could be attached to the carriage seat when needed. Some are attached permanently while others are attached to a shifting rail or folded down when not in use.

Lead bars: a three-part unit fixed to the pole hook for attachment of the leaders, or front horses. The main bar is attached to a pair of swingletrees. See also *swingletree.*

Light: window. *Quarter lights* are windows in quarter panels; *drop lights* are windows that can be raised and lowered.

Linchpin: a metal pin securing the wheel at the end of the axle to prevent it from slipping off the axle.

Nut: a metal block with a threaded hole for screwing onto a bolt. *Axle nut:* the nut used in place of a linchpin to secure the wheel to the end of the axle. *Hub nut:* see *hub. Prop nut:* the nut used on the end of the bolt that secures the bows of a folding hood.

Pageboard: a small board at the rear of a coach for the footmen to stand or sit upon.

Painted carpet, oil carpet or **oilcloth:** a heavy, painted cloth, often with decorative painting or stencilling, that was used to cover the floor of a carriage.

Panel: one of the wooden sections used in the construction of a carriage body, as in *lower* and *upper quarter panel, door panel, boot panel.*

Perch: piece of timber, iron or steel, or combination of metal and wood, connecting the front and rear axles. Also called a *reach.*

Pillar: the upright framework of a carriage body. *Door pillars* are used in an enclosed carriage; *standing* or *fixed pillars* support the roof of a wagonette or omnibus, in contrast to the movable bows that support collapsible or removable tops.

Pole: a long piece of timber connected to the carriage, extending between the horses and used as a lever to guide the carriage.

Postilion: a method of driving coachman-driven vehicles on formal occasions in which the driver guides the horses while riding astride the near-side horse, that is, the horse on the left.

Pump handles: bars of wood or iron attached to the bottom side or rocker of a vehicle body at the back end, acting as a support for the rear of the body.

Raved: ribbed, as in the ribbed side panels of a carriage or sleigh.

Reach: see *perch.*

Reins or **ribbons:** the leather straps attached to the horse's bit that are held by the driver and used to guide and control the horse; *rein guides* are small brackets attached to the dash that keep the reins in place.

Robin: a round band of iron covered with leather or India rubber, used to connect side and cross springs.

Rub iron: a metal plate attached to the side of a vehicle to prevent a turning wheel from chafing the body. A *roller rub iron* has a loose rolling metal cylinder and is generally used in conjunction with rubber tires to keep a turning wheel from binding.

Runners: long, parallel strips of iron or wood faced with iron upon which a sleigh slides along snow and ice. See also *bobs.*

Seat: a board, bench or other platform for seating for driver or passenger. A *dickey seat* is the front seat for the coachman, distinct from the body, or the rear seat behind a carriage; a *jump seat,* or child's seat, is a small collapsible seat that folds out from a storage compartment in the carriage interior; a *knifeboard seat* is a bench-like seat placed longitudinally in a wagonette or omnibus; a *rumble seat* is a seat for the groom and is attached to the rear of certain carriages.

Seat riser: one of the wood or metal supports that elevate a seat above the body or floor of a vehicle.

Shackle: a metal loop made in various shapes, used to connect separate springs or sections of a spring.

Shafts: two wooden poles attached to the gearing of a carriage, between which the horse is secured.

Shoulder: the part of the spoke bearing against the hub.

Singletree: see *swingletree.*

Slide: a small plate of wood or carved ivory that provides a pad or a guard for the window or glass lifter to prevent it from wearing or catching on the wood or broadlace below the window.

Snipebill: see *kingpin.*

Splinter bar: the rigid crossbar at the front of a vehicle, to which the traces of a pair of horses are attached.

Spring block: a small block attached to the axle or other part of the gear to support a spring.

Squab: quilted, stuffed lining for the backs and quarters of interior trim.

Stable shutter: an ornamental paneled frame, used as a substitute for glass, to prevent light and dust from entering a carriage.

Steps: fixed or hinged brackets used by drivers and passengers to enter or exit a vehicle. *Branched steps* have long and short *step pads,* or *step plates,* attached to a single, fixed iron shank; *book steps* are folding steps that are attached by a hinge and unfold automatically with the action of the door; other vehicles have folding steps that slide out or are manually lifted from underneath the vehicle or from its interior.

Studs: a configuration of a tire iron on a carriage wheel in which large, flat-headed bolts are driven through the tire into the wooden felloes.

Swingletree: a short bar attached to the splinter bar (or to the crossbar shafts), to which traces are attached. "Tree" refers to the material used, which is wood; "swingle" to the swinging motion. The pivoting of this section reduces friction against the chest of the horse while in draft; *singletree,* synonymous with swingletree, is a corruption of the term.

Thoroughbrace: long leather straps stitched together, running under the body of a carriage, used to suspend and support it.

Tire iron: the iron band surrounding the rim of a wheel to which it is nailed, screwed, riveted or shrunk; its purpose is to strengthen the wheel and protect the wooden felloes from wear. The tire iron, when applied hot, cools, and in shrinking drives the spoke tenons into the hub and the spoke dowels into the felloes.

Toeboard: a board attached to the brackets of heavy coaches, which serves as a footrest for the driver.

Trace: that part of the harness by which the horse draws the vehicle.

Transom: a bar of wood to which the front of a perch is attached, resting on the front of the axle, to which it is attached by the king bolt.

Trim: the upholstery, carpeting, accessories and decoration of a carriage interior, including seat upholstery and wall and ceiling covering. Fabrics used for trim range from plain broadcloth, leather or coarsely woven coaching carpet in wool (sometimes called "tapestry") to elegant brocades and velvets in more lavish vehicles. In pleasure or sporting vehicles, for example, Bedford cord, a corduroy-like material, might be used.

Turnout: the complete assemblage of vehicle, accoutrements, horse(s), harness, costume of driver, coachmen and grooms, the aim of which was to create a pleasing and harmonious effect as prescribed by contemporary fashion and taste. Each type of vehicle had its appropriate requisites for the manner in which it was "turned out."

Undercarriage: see *gear*.

Whiffletree: see *swingletree*.

Whip: (1) an experienced driver; (2) a slender instrument of woven gut, wood or other materials with a lash or thong attached to the end to urge, direct or discipline a horse.

An excellent source of more extensive terms and detailed definitions can be found in Berkebile's *Carriage Terminology: An Historical Dictionary*, included in Further Readings.

Further Readings

Adams, William Bridges. *English Pleasure Carriages: their Origin, History, Varieties, Materials, Construction.* . . . London: Charles Knight & Co., 1837.

Berkebile, Don H. *Carriage Terminology: An Historical Dictionary.* Washington, D.C.: Smithsonian Institution Press & Liberty Cap Books, 1978.

The Coach-Makers' Illustrated Handbook. Philadelphia: I. D. Ware, 1872.

Ditzel, Paul C. *Fire Engines, Firefighters.* New York: Crown Publishers, Inc., 1976.

Dunbar, Seymour. *A History of Travel in America.* Indianapolis: The Bobbs-Merrill Company, 1915.

Felton, William. *A treatise on carriages, comprehending coaches, chariots, phaetons, curricles, gigs, whiskeys, etc. together with their proper harness.* . . . London: printed for and sold by the author, 1796.

Fitz-Gerald, William N. *The Carriage Trimmers' Manual and Guide Book.* New York: William N. Fitz-Gerald, 1881.

Gannon, William Louis. *Carriage, Coach and Wagon: the Design and Decoration of American Horse-Drawn Vehicles.* Unpublished Ph.D. dissertation, State University of Iowa, 1960. Ann Arbor, Michigan: University Microfilm, Inc., 1960.

Garland, James A. *The Private Stable: its Establishment, Management and Appointment.* Boston: Little, Brown and Co., 1903.

Gilbey, Sir Walter. *Early Carriages and Roads.* London: Vinton & Co., 1903.

————. *Modern Carriages.* London: Vinton & Co., 1905.

Holmes, Oliver W. and Peter T. Rohrbach. *Stagecoach East.* Washington, D.C.: Smithsonian Institution Press, 1983.

Holzman, Robert. *The Romance of Firefighting.* New York: Harper and Brothers, 1956.

McCausland, Hugh. *The English Carriage.* London: The Batchworth Press, 1948.

Moore, Henry Charles. *Omnibuses and Cabs; their Origin and History.* London: Chapman & Hall, Ltd., 1902.

Rives, Reginald W. *The Coaching Club; Its History, Records and Activities.* Privately Printed, 1935.

Rogers, Fairman. *A Manual of Coaching.* Philadelphia: J. B. Lippincott, 1899.

Shone, A. B. *A Century and a Half of Amateur Driving.* London: J. Allen, Ltd., 1955.

Stratton, Ezra M. *The World on Wheels, or Carriages, with their Historical Associations from the Earliest to the Present Time.* New York: Ezra M. Stratton, 1878.

Straus, Ralph. *Carriages & Coaches.* London: Martin Secker, 1912.

Tarr, Laszlo. *The History of Carriages.* New York: Arco Publishing Co., Inc., 1959.

Thrupp, G. A. *The History of Coaches.* London: Kerby & Endean, 1877.

Underhill, Francis T. *Driving for Pleasure; or the Harness Stable and its Appointments.* New York: D. Appleton and Company, 1896.

Ware, Francis M. *Driving.* New York: Doubleday, Page & Company, 1903.

Wilson, Violet A. *The Coaching Era.* New York: E. P. Dutton & Company, 1922; London: John Lane, The Bodley Head Ltd., n.d.

Index to Vehicles

By Name and by Catalog Number

Basket phaeton, 38, 39
Basket wagon, 10
Berlin coach, 3
Booby hut, 60
Break
 Roof-seat, 43
 Skeleton, 45
 Wagonette, 42
Britzka, 6
Brougham
 Circular Front, 29
 Station, 31
 Summer, 30
Buckboard phaeton, 37
Buggy.
 Doctor's, 15
 Hooded, 13
 Stanhope, 14
Butcher's wagon, 64

Cab, hansom, 74
Cabriolet, 47
Cart, east williston, 53
Chaise, 8
Chaise, four-wheel, 9
Chariot D'Orsay, 27
Circular front brougham, 29
Circular front coupé, 28
Coach, 24, 25, 71
Coach
 Berlin, 3
 Concord, 70
 Private road, 44
 State, 4
 Town, 26
 Wells Fargo, 69
Commissary wagon, Laska, 46
Concord coach, 70
Coupé rockaway, 22
Coupé, circular front, 28
Curricle, 48, 49
Cutter, 58

Democrat wagon, 18
Doctor's buggy, 15
Dogcart, 50
Dos-a-dos phaeton, 40

East williston cart, 53

Four-wheel chaise, 9

George IV phaeton, 34
Gig, 1, 7, 51
Gooseneck pumper, side-stroke, 77
Grand duc, 5
Gypsy wagon, 23

Hack passenger wagon, 73
Hansom cab, 74
Hooded buggy, 13
Hose carriage, 78
Hose carriage, parade, 80

Inside car, 52

Laska commissary wagon, 46

Mail phaeton, 35
Mail wagon, 65
Market wagon, 61
Mountain wagon, 72

Omnibus, 76
Omnibus, station, 75

Panel boot victoria, 32
Parade hose carriage, 80
Peddler's wagon, 63
Perfume wagon, 68
Phaeton
 Basket, 38, 39
 Buckboard, 37
 Dos-a-dos, 40
 George IV, 34
 Mail, 35
 Slat-side mountain, 41
 Spider, 36
Platform wagon, 19
Pleasure wagon, 11, 12
Popcorn wagon, 67
Private road coach, 44
Pumper, side-stroke gooseneck, 77
Pumper, steam, 79

Road wagon, 16
Rockaway, 21
Rockaway, coupé, 22
Roof-seat break, 43

Side-stroke gooseneck pumper, 77
Skeleton break, 45
Skeleton wagon, 17
Slat-side mountain phaeton, 41
Sleigh, 2, 54, 55, 56, 57
Sleigh, vis-a-vis, 59

Sleigh (booby hut), 60
Sleigh (cutter), 58
Spider phaeton, 36
Stanhope buggy, 14
Standard Oil wagon, 62
State coach, 4
Station brougham, 31
Station omnibus, 75
Steam pumper, 79
Summer brougham, 30
Summer vis-a-vis, 33

Tea wagon, 66
Town coach, 26
Trap, 20

Victoria, panel boot, 32
Vis-a-vis sleigh, 59
Vis-a-vis, summer, 33

Wagon
 Basket, 10
 Butcher's, 64
 Democrat, 18
 Gypsy, 23
 Hack passenger, 73
 Laska commissary, 46
 Mail, 65
 Market, 61
 Mountain, 72
 Peddler's, 63
 Perfume, 68
 Platform, 19
 Pleasure, 11, 12
 Popcorn, 67
 Road, 16
 Skeleton, 17
 Standard Oil, 62
 Tea, 66
Wagonette break, 42
Wells Fargo coach, 69